The Quick and Easy Japanese Cookbook

The Quick and Easy Japanese Cookbook

Great Recipes from Japan's Favorite TV Cooking Show Host

Katsuyo Kobayashi

KODANSHA INTERNATIONAL
Tokyo • New York • London

NOTE:

Weights and measures differ in Japan, the U.S., and England. For the sake of convenience, this book uses the measuring cup and spoon considered standard in Japan. For the reader's convenience, the standards in the three countries are as follows:

	Cup	Tablespoon	Teaspoon
Japan	200 cc	15 cc	5 cc
U.S.	240 cc	15 cc	5 cc
England	280 cc	19 cc	6 cc

(The cup referred to under the heading of England is the English breakfast-cup.)

1 pound (16 oz) = 450 g   1 oz = 30 g

1 inch = $2\frac{1}{2}$ cm   2 inches = 5 cm

300°F = 150°C   325°F = 160°C   350°F = 180°C   400°F = 200°C

Distributed in the United States by Kodansha America, Inc., and in the United Kingdom and continental Europe by Kodansha Europe Ltd.

Published by Kodansha International Ltd., 17–14 Otowa 1-chome, Bunkyo-ku, Tokyo 112–8652, and Kodansha America, Inc.

ISBN-13: 978–4–7700–2504–3
ISBN-10: 4–7700–2504–1

First edition, 2000
10 09 08 07 06   10 9 8 7 6

Library of Congress Cataloging-in-Publication data available

www.kodansha-intl.com

C O N T E N T S

VEGETABLES

EGGS

TOFU

RICE/NOODLES

SOUPS

Basic Techniques

I N T R O D U C T I O N

Many people in the West have the impression that Japanese cooking is difficult and time-consuming, although this is far from true. My aim in this book is to introduce a number of dishes that are delicious but easy to prepare.

The variety of the recipes given here may come as a surprise. People who are not familiar with Japanese family-style food may think that the cuisine consists of just the sushi and sukiyaki that are so popular in restaurants around the world. In fact, home cooking covers a very wide range of ingredients and cooking methods. In addition, influences from Asia and Europe have been adapted to the Japanese palate, and made an integral part of the national cuisine.

Almost all the ingredients in this book are readily available outside Japan. Readers may want to buy in a few basic flavorings such as soy sauce and miso paste that last a long time and are used in various recipes. For any items that may be less familiar, I have taken care to note possible alternatives.

I hope that this cookbook helps people around the world to discover how easy it is to make Japanese food at home, and how satisfying and delicious the results can be.

Mixed Rice with Shrimp and Vegetables

15 | Serves 4
353 cal/serving

ACTIVE TIME 15 min.
TOTAL TIME 40 min.

2 cups uncooked rice

2 ⅖ cups water

1 small carrot

1 section (7 oz/200 g) *renkon* lotus root (or boiled bamboo shoot)

8 to 10 large shrimp

1 Tbsp rice vinegar + 4 Tbsp rice vinegar

8 to 10 dried shiitake mushrooms

1 Tbsp sesame oil

1½ Tbsp soy sauce

1½ Tbsp sugar + 1 Tbsp sugar

1 Tbsp saké

1 tsp salt

4-inch (10-cm) strip of dried *konbu* kelp, (optional)

2 to 3 stalks *mitsuba* trefoil (or Italian parsley)

LOTUS ROOT

1. Wash the rice, add the water, and set aside.

2. Slice the carrot into thin rounds and then into matchsticks. If the lotus root is thick, cut lengthwise into fourths. Cut into thin slices, and soak briefly in cold water to remove any astringency.

3. In a small pan of boiling water, cook shrimp until they turn color. Add 1 tablespoon vinegar to the pan for flavoring, stir briefly, and remove from heat. Drain and shell shrimp, leaving tails still attached.

4. Reconstitute shiitake mushrooms by soaking them in warm water for a few minutes until they soften. Drain, reserving the mushroom water, and discard the stems. Squeeze the remaining water from the mushrooms, place in a small pan, and sauté both sides well in sesame oil.

Leftover mushroom water is delicious when added to miso soup or any other kind of soup.

5. Add soy sauce, 1½ tablespoons sugar, and just enough mushroom water to cover, and simmer over medium heat until most of the water evaporates. Cool and cut mushrooms into thin strips.

6. Combine saké, salt, 4 tablespoons rice vinegar, and 1 tablespoon sugar. Remove 5 tablespoons water from the uncooked rice, replace with this mixture, and stir briefly. Arrange the kelp, carrot, and lotus root evenly over the rice, add shrimp, and cook the rice (see page 89). Allow the rice to steam another 10 minutes after it is cooked.

7. Gently mix the rice so the ingredients are spread evenly, remove the kelp, and serve with a garnish of chopped trefoil.

Clams Steamed in Saké

Serves 2–4
39 cal/serving

8 to 12 fresh *hamaguri* hard clams (or mussels)

2 Tbsp saké

1 thin green *bannonegi* onion, or chives (optional)

soy sauce to taste (optional)

Good as a side dish with spaghetti. Also delicious with garlic toast and a glass of wine.

1. Place clams in a large bowl of cold water and remove any dirt with your hands (if using mussels, rinse and remove beards).

2. Place clams in a pan, sprinkle with saké, cover the pan, and steam over high heat about 5 minutes until all clams are completely open. (Discard any that do not open.)

3. Just before serving, garnish with finely chopped green onion and drizzle with soy sauce.

If you buy your clams from a fish market, they may need to be cleaned more thoroughly. Soak in water slightly less salty than seawater before doing Step 1.

Seafood Salad

Serves 2–4
74 cal/serving

2 to 3 cooked octopus legs (or 7 oz/200 g boiled squid)

1 to 2 cucumbers

1 small red bell pepper

1 small yellow bell pepper

½ tsp salt

1 Tbsp rice vinegar

1 Tbsp olive oil

oregano, sweet basil, and ground black pepper to taste

1. Slice octopus legs into thin, bite-sized rounds.

2. Slice cucumbers thinly on the diagonal and cut vertically into matchsticks. Cut red and yellow peppers in half lengthwise, remove caps and seeds, and cut horizontally into thin strips.

3. Place octopus, cucumbers, and bell peppers in a bowl of ice water for 5 minutes to crisp. Drain, pat dry with paper towels, and place in a salad bowl.

4. Sprinkle salad with salt and drizzle with vinegar and olive oil, in that order. Toss briefly and garnish with a sprinkling of oregano, basil, and ground black pepper.

Soaking in ice water makes the cucumbers crispier and mellows the taste of the peppers.

Shrimp and Celery Salad with Ginger Dressing

Serves 3–4
112 cal/serving

10 to 12 shrimp
2 celery stalks
leaves of 2 celery stalks
1 Tbsp rice vinegar

2 tsp sugar
$\frac{1}{2}$ to 1 tsp salt
$\frac{1}{2}$ to 1 tsp fresh ginger juice
(or 1 tsp minced ginger)

GINGER

1. Devein shrimp and place them in lightly salted boiling water. Cook over high heat until they turn color. Remove from water and shell, then cut each in half lengthwise and pat dry.

2. Remove celery strings and cut stalks into 3-inch (7- to 8-cm) lengths. Cut these lengthwise into very thin slices and place in a bowl of cold water to crisp.

3. Chop celery leaves very finely.

4. In a salad bowl, combine vinegar, sugar, salt, and ginger juice. Add shrimp, celery stalks, and celery leaves, in that order. Toss and serve.

Boiling shrimp in the shell makes them more flavorful and helps them keep their shape. To devein fresh shrimp, make a small cut along the center of the back and use a toothpick to remove the vein.

To make ginger juice, grate ginger and squeeze out the juice with your fingers. For 1 teaspoon of juice, you will need a knob of fresh ginger about 1 inch (2 $\frac{1}{2}$ cm) long.

15

Salmon Simmered in Wine

15 | **Serves 4** | 415 cal/serving

4 salmon fillets (3 ½ oz/100 g each)
1 to 2 celery stalks, with leaves
1 pickled cucumber
4 Tbsp mayonnaise
2 Tbsp milk

½ cup white wine
1 cup water
1 bay leaf
12 to 16 cherry tomatoes
½ lemon, cut into wedges

1. Remove any bones from salmon fillets.

2. Remove celery strings and cut stalks and leaves into 2-inch (5-cm) lengths. Cut the wider parts of the stalks lengthwise into 2 or 3 pieces.

3. Chop the pickled cucumber finely, and make the tartar sauce by combining it with mayonnaise and milk and stirring.

4. In a fry pan, combine wine, water, bay leaf, and celery stalks (but not leaves) and cook on high heat. When the mixture comes to a boil, arrange salmon fillets in the pan, sprinkle with celery leaves, cover, and simmer over medium heat until cooked through, about 10 minutes. Just before serving, add cherry tomatoes and heat briefly.

5. Serve on individual plates with tartar sauce and a wedge of lemon.

Add cherry tomatoes just at the very end, and heat briefly.

Quick-Simmered Mackerel with Miso Sauce

20 | **Serves 4** | 179 cal/serving

4 *saba* mackerel fillets (each 6 oz/160 g)
1 *gobo* burdock root, unpeeled
1 Tbsp *mirin* + 2 Tbsp *mirin*
1 Tbsp soy sauce
generous ½ cup saké

½ cup water + ¼ cup water
1 generous Tbsp miso paste
 (red, if possible)
1 Tbsp sugar
mustard to taste

BURDOCK ROOT

1. Cut each fillet in two and pat dry. Make several incisions on the skin side of the fish.

2. Scrub the burdock root thoroughly and cut into 2-inch (5-cm) lengths. Parboil 5 to 10 minutes to soften.

3. In a shallow pan, combine 1 tablespoon mirin, soy sauce, saké, and ½ cup water, and bring to a boil. Add fish skin-side up in a single layer, and slip burdock in between pieces of fish.

4. Cover pan and simmer over medium-high heat for about 10 minutes, basting occasionally.

5. When most of the liquid has evaporated and the fish is cooked through, make the miso sauce in a small bowl by combining and mixing miso paste, sugar, 2 tablespoons mirin, and ¼ cup water. Add this sauce to the pan and simmer about 3 more minutes, basting occasionally. Remove pan from heat.

6. Arrange fish and burdock on individual plates. Briefly reheat the sauce, spoon it over the fish, add a dab of mustard, and serve.

After adding miso sauce, simmer while basting occasionally and tilting the pot so the liquid is evenly distributed.

If burdock is not readily available, try okra, Brussels sprouts, or shiitake mushrooms instead.

Substitute 1 tablespoon saké + 1 teaspoon sugar for each tablespoon of mirin.

Cod with Tofu

20 | **Serves 4** | 220 cal/serving

4 slightly salted cod fillets (each 4½ oz/130 g)

2 cakes tofu (firm, if possible)

8- to 10-inch (20- to 25-cm) piece of daikon

3 cups *dashi* stock

3 Tbsp saké

3 Tbsp light-colored (*usukuchi*) soy sauce

1 Tbsp *mirin*

pinch of salt

shichimi togarashi red pepper, or red chili flakes (optional)

Japanese *yuzu* citron peel (optional)

Blanching the cod improves the taste and makes it milder. Once the surface is sealed, place in a colander and remove the bones.

1. Cut each fillet into 3 pieces. Blanch a few seconds in boiling water, drain, and remove any bones.

2. Cut each cake of tofu into 8 pieces.

3. Grate the daikon and place in a colander to drain

4. Place the dashi stock (see page 90) in a pan, add cod and tofu, and bring to a boil over high heat. Add saké, soy sauce, mirin, and salt, and bring to a boil once more. Lower heat a little and simmer a minute or so, until tofu is heated through.

5. Add the grated daikon and mix, and let it come to a boil. Cover the pan, remove from heat, and let it steam about 2 minutes.

6. Serve with a sprinkling of red pepper and tiny shavings of citron peel.

For those who are buying fish in Japan, salt cod is known as shiodara, and fresh cod is namadara. If you are using fresh cod, add a generous pinch of salt.

If you do not have light-colored soy sauce on hand, use 1 tablespoon soy sauce + 1½ teaspoons salt instead. As a substitute for mirin, use 1 tablespoon saké + 1 teaspoon sugar.

Breaded Shrimp

30 | **Serves 4** | 216 cal/serving

12 medium or 8 large shrimp

all-purpose flour

1 egg, beaten

breadcrumbs

vegetable oil for deep-frying

lettuce leaves

cherry tomatoes

½ lemon, cut into wedges

mayonnaise to taste

Worcestershire sauce to taste

With the tip of a sharp knife, make a few incisions on the underside and gently pull shrimp straight.

1. Shell shrimp, leaving tails still attached, and devein. Make 3 or 4 incisions on the underside of each to prevent curling, and straighten shrimp by gently pulling until you feel a slight give. Pat dry with paper towels.

2. Sprinkle shrimp with flour, dip into beaten egg, and coat with breadcrumbs.

3. Heat oil to medium (350°F/170° to 180°C) and deep-fry shrimp until golden brown. Remove and drain on a rack.

4. Arrange on individual plates with a mound of lettuce cut into thin strips, cherry tomatoes, and a lemon wedge. Serve with mayonnaise or Worcestershire sauce.

Check the oil temperature by stirring the oil and dropping a little batter into it. If the batter sinks halfway down and rises back up to the surface, the temperature is just right.

If you prefer tartar sauce, make it by combining 2 tablespoons mayonnaise, 1 tablespoon milk, and a little finely chopped pickled cucumber.

Salt-Grilled Whole Fish

 **Serves 4**
253 cal/serving

4 *sanma* Pacific saury, *nijimasu* rainbow trout, *aji* horse mackerel, salmon fillets, or any other small fish

salt to season fish

5-inch (12-cm) piece of daikon, grated (optional)

2 Japanese *sudachi* limes (or lemon wedges)

soy sauce to taste

To season fish evenly with salt, sprinkle salt from 8 inches (20 cm) above. Turn fish over and repeat on the other side. Do not rub fish with salt.

1. Buy fish that has been cleaned and scaled (the heads and tails may be left on or removed). Rinse fish and pat dry with paper towels. Sprinkle salt on both sides of the fish, and set aside for 5 to 10 minutes.

2. In a broiler, set fish on a rack with a pan beneath to catch drips. Broil 7 or 8 minutes, until top side is golden.

3. Peel and grate the daikon, and place in a colander to drain.

4. Arrange fish on individual plates and garnish with a small mound of grated daikon and half a Japanese lime. Set soy sauce out on the table for people to drizzle over the fish and daikon as they like.

This dish can also be made in a nonstick fry pan. To do this, do not sprinkle salt onto the fish, but instead soak fish in salted water for 20 to 30 minutes before cooking, and pat dry. Heat a fry pan to very hot. Add fish and lower heat to medium. Fry until golden brown, turn over, and cook the other side.

Foil-Baked Cod with Mushrooms

 **Serves 4**
113 cal/serving

Almost any kind of fish is delicious done this way. Try salmon or a white fish such as flounder or halibut (in Japan, look for karei or hirame). Sea bass (suzuki) is also good.

3 1/2 oz (100 g) fresh mushrooms, any kind (button, shiitake, *shimeji*, etc.)

vegetable oil

4 fresh cod fillets (each 4 1/2 oz/130 g)

salt and ground black pepper to taste

4 tsp saké

4 tsp butter

1/2 lemon, cut into wedges

soy sauce to taste

Cod is often sold slightly salted in Japan. To remove the salt, soak fish for 5 to 10 minutes in water slightly saltier than seawater.

1. Trim off the hard ends of the mushroom stems and, depending on the type used, either separate mushrooms into small clusters or cut caps into thin strips.

2. Prepare four 8-inch (20-cm) squares of aluminum foil and spread a little vegetable oil in the center of each square. Place a piece of fish on the foil and season with salt and pepper. Add one-fourth of the mushrooms, sprinkle fish with 1 teaspoon saké, and top with 1 teaspoon butter. Make four of these foil packets.

3. Seal each packet by bringing two edges of the foil together and folding over twice. Then fold the other edges in toward the center.

4. Preheat oven to very high, or 480°F (250°C) and bake 10 to 15 minutes. If using a toaster oven, cook two packets at a time for 10 to 15 minutes.

5. Serve the fish in the foil. Garnish with a wedge of lemon and drizzle with soy sauce.

Bring the longer edges of the foil together, and fold over the fish twice. Fold the shorter ends in toward the center.

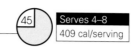

Assorted Tempura

(45) **Serves 4–8**
409 cal/serving

8 large shrimp

1 squid

4 *kisu* whiting (or very thin fillets of any white fish)

1 small carrot

2 oz (50 g) green beans

7 oz (200 g) section of *renkon* lotus root

10 oz (280 g) *satsumaimo* sweet potato

FOR THE BATTER

1 egg, beaten

1 scant cup ice water

1 cup all-purpose flour

oil for deep-frying

FOR THE DIPPING SAUCE

2 cups dashi stock

2 Tbsp *mirin* (or 2 Tbsp saké + 2 tsp sugar)

4 Tbsp light-colored (*usukuchi*) soy sauce (or 4 Tbsp regular soy sauce + 2 pinches of salt)

1 Tbsp soy sauce

6-inch (15-cm) piece of daikon, grated

1 knob fresh ginger, grated

> Any of these ingredients will also work well in tempura: onion, potato, bell pepper, thinly sliced kabocha squash, fresh shiitake or other mushrooms, or whole okra.

> Check the oil temperature by stirring the oil and dropping a little batter into it. If the batter sinks halfway down and rises back up to the surface, the temperature is just right.

Spread ingredients out evenly in the pan, starting from the center. Once the batter has set, pick up a piece and expose it to the air for a moment.

1. Shell shrimp, leaving tails still attached, and devein. Make 3 or 4 incisions on the underside of each to prevent curling, and gently pull straight.

2. Gut the squid and remove the thin membranous skin. Cut squid in half lengthwise and then into strips ¾ inch (2 cm) wide.

3. Lightly rinse the whiting.

4. Cut carrot into ¼-inch (5-mm) rounds. String the green beans and cut into 2 or 3 sections.

5. Peel lotus root and sweet potato and cut into ¼-inch (5-mm) rounds. Place both in lightly salted water for a few minutes.

6. Make the batter by adding enough ice water to the beaten egg to make one cup. Add the flour and mix through lightly.

> When deep-frying, let ingredients cook undisturbed until the batter sets. Then pick them up with cooking chopsticks or tongs and expose them to the air for a moment before returning them to the oil. By "airing" it, you can make crispy tempura without having to use a lot of oil.

7. In a fry pan, heat the oil to 350°F (170° to 180°C). Pat all ingredients dry with paper towels so they are ready to be dipped in batter and deep-fried. Start with the lotus root and sweet potato, since they take longest to cook, and follow with the seafood. Before dipping the squid in batter, sprinkle both sides lightly with flour to prevent splashing. Cook the carrot and beans last (dip beans in small batches, rather than singly).

   (Dip each ingredient quickly in the batter like a bird diving for food, and immediately deep-fry. Add ingredients to the pan one at a time, spreading them out evenly, without any overlap. Since the oil temperature will drop after each new ingredient is added, turn heat a bit higher just after adding, then adjust down as the temperature rises again.)

> Occasionally use a strainer to remove small pieces of batter from the oil, to keep them from burning.

8. As soon as ingredients are cooked and crispy, remove from the pan and place on a rack to drain. Before serving, arrange attractively on a large plate.

9. Make the dipping sauce by combining dashi stock, mirin, light-colored soy sauce, and regular soy sauce, and bringing them to a boil over high heat. Place a little grated daikon and grated ginger in small individual bowls and ladle dipping sauce into the bowls. (Each person takes one piece of tempura at a time, dipping it into his or her own small bowl before eating.)

> When ingredients are done, the frying sounds grow quieter and the ingredients become lighter. Shake off all excess oil and drain ingredients by standing them upright on a rack in rows.

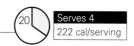

Sweet-and-Sour Fish

20 | Serves 4
222 cal/serving

5 to 6 dried shiitake mushrooms

1 boiled bamboo shoot (7 oz/200 g)

½ carrot

½ onion

1 knob (1 inch/2½ cm) fresh ginger

4 to 5 thin green *bannonegi* onions (or chives)

4 fillets of flounder, or cod, or any other white fish (each 5 oz/140 g)

potato starch for dusting fish + 1 Tbsp potato starch dissolved in 1 Tbsp water

vegetable oil for deep-frying

½ cup water

1 Tbsp ketchup

1 Tbsp rice vinegar

1 Tbsp sugar

1 Tbsp saké

2 Tbsp light-colored (*usukuchi*) soy sauce (or 2 tsp regular soy sauce + 1 tsp salt)

½ tsp sesame oil

THIN GREEN ONIONS

1. Reconstitute shiitake mushrooms by soaking them in warm water for 10 minutes until they soften. Drain. Discard stems and cut caps into thin strips. Cut the bamboo shoot and the carrot into thin slices and then into matchsticks. Slice the onion finely. Cut the ginger into thin strips. Cut green onions into 1-inch (2½-cm) lengths.

2. Cut the fish into bite-sized pieces and dust with potato starch. In a wok or fry pan, heat the oil to medium (see page 19, note to "Breaded Shrimp"), add the fish, and deep-fry until cooked through and crispy. Remove from heat and arrange fish on a dish.

3. In a small pan, combine water, ketchup, vinegar, sugar, saké, and soy sauce. Add mushrooms, bamboo shoot, carrot, onion, and ginger, bring to a boil, and cook until the carrot softens. Stir in the dissolved potato starch and remove from heat as soon as the mixture thickens and glazes.

4. Add green onions and sesame oil, and mix quickly. Pour the sauce over the fish and serve immediately.

Quick-Simmered Fish with Saké and Ginger

15 | Serves 4
126 cal/serving

4 fillets of *karei* flounder, or any white fish (each 6 oz/160 g)

1 knob fresh ginger, unpeeled

12 *shishito* sweet green peppers (or 2 bell peppers)

½ cup saké

½ cup water

3 to 4 Tbsp soy sauce

3 to 4 Tbsp mirin (or 3 to 4 Tbsp saké + 1 Tbsp sugar)

1 Tbsp sugar

Baste the fish evenly with stock. This dish should be cooked over high heat, as a low flame makes the fish taste "fishy."

1. Pat the fish dry and make several light incisions in the skin on both sides.

2. Slice the ginger thinly against the grain. Trim the stems of the shishito peppers.

3. Slightly wet a medium pan (to prevent sticking), and combine saké, water, soy sauce, mirin, and sugar, and bring to a boil over medium heat. Add fish, cover the pan, and cook 7 to 10 minutes over high heat, basting occasionally. Add peppers after 5 minutes and simmer with the fish for the last few minutes.

4. Serve, ladling sauce over the fish and peppers.

If using bell peppers, cut lengthwise into 4 to 6 pieces.

Fragrant Chicken Nuggets and Long Onions

(15) | Serves 2–4
345 cal/serving

2 boneless chicken thighs
2 long green *naganegi* onions (or 1 onion)
2 Tbsp miso paste
2 Tbsp *mirin* (or honey)
2 Tbsp saké

1 tsp sesame oil
Japanese *sansho* pepper (or *shichimi toga-rashi* red pepper, or red chili flakes)
vegetable oil for frying
salt to taste

Trim any excess fat from the chicken.

If you don't have any miso on hand, you can substitute 2 tablespoons soy sauce.

1. Trim off excess fat and cut the chicken into bite-sized pieces. Cut the long onion into 1½-inch (4-cm) lengths.

2. In a bowl, combine miso paste, mirin, saké, sesame oil, and Japanese pepper, and mix well.

3. Heat a little oil in a fry pan, and when it gets quite hot, add the chicken, skin-side down, and sauté over medium-high heat until skin is brown and crisp. Turn over and add long onions wherever there is room. Continue to sauté until cooked through.

4. Pour the miso mixture directly over the chicken, turn heat down to medium, and continue cooking until the sauce glazes and thickens. Sprinkle onions with salt and Japanese pepper to taste. Remove from heat, arrange chicken and onions on a plate, and serve.

LONG GREEN ONIONS

Japanese Pan-Fried Chicken

15 | Serves 4
228 cal/serving

2 to 3 boneless chicken thighs

8 fresh shiitake mushrooms

8 *shishito* sweet green peppers (or 3 small bell peppers)

2 to 3 Tbsp *mirin* (or 2 to 3 Tbsp saké + 2 tsp sugar)

2 to 3 Tbsp soy sauce

Japanese *sansho* pepper (optional)

shichimi togarashi red pepper, or red chili flakes (optional)

1. Trim off any excess fat from the chicken.

2. Cut off hard stems of the mushrooms, and cut each mushroom in half or into quarters. If using bell peppers, remove caps and seeds, and cut lengthwise into 4 to 6 pieces.

3. Make the sauce by combining mirin and soy sauce, and set aside.

4. Heat a nonstick fry pan until very hot. Place chicken skin-side down and fry over medium-high heat until the skin starts to crisp and turn golden brown. Turn chicken over and brown the other side. Add shiitake and green peppers to the pan.

5. When the meat is just cooked through, add the sauce. Turn chicken and vegetables repeatedly, to develop the flavor.

6. When sauce thickens, remove chicken from the pan and cut into easy-to-eat pieces. Arrange attractively on a dish with mushrooms and peppers. Serve hot, setting out sansho pepper and shichimi togarashi red pepper on the table as optional seasonings.

Banbanji Chilled Sesame Chicken

20 | Serves 2–4
243 cal/serving

2 chicken breasts (9 oz/250 g)

a pinch of salt

1 pack (9 oz/250 g) bean sprouts

2 cucumbers

¾ cup roasted white sesame seeds

3 Tbsp soy sauce

3 Tbsp *mirin* (or 3 Tbsp saké + 1 Tbsp sugar)

3 Tbsp rice vinegar

12 cherry tomatoes, halved

Adding the reserved chicken stock to the sauce lightens the taste of the sesame.

Be sure to grind sesame seeds thoroughly.

1. Place chicken in a small pan of lightly salted boiling water and boil for about 10 minutes. Allow to cool in the water. Remove chicken, reserving the stock. When cool, tear chicken into long thin strips by hand.

2. In a separate pan, blanch bean sprouts, rinse immediately in cold water, and drain.

3. Slice cucumbers thinly on the diagonal, and cut vertically into matchsticks.

4. Make the sauce by grinding the sesame seeds with a Japanese-style mortar and pestle, or in a grinder or food processor. Add soy sauce, mirin, and vinegar, and mix in some of the reserved stock, a little at a time, stirring until the mixture becomes smooth.

5. Arrange bean sprouts, cucumbers, and chicken on a plate. Dress with sesame sauce and serve with cherry tomatoes.

Quick-Fried Liver with *Nira* Chinese Chives

20 | Serves 4
101 cal/serving

7 oz (200 g) chicken or pork livers
1 clove garlic
1 bunch (3 ½ oz/100 g) *nira* Chinese chives
2 Tbsp vegetable oil for frying

2 Tbsp soy sauce
1 Tbsp saké
ground black pepper to taste

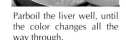

Parboil the liver well, until the color changes all the way through.

1. Rinse livers gently under running water and cut into bite-sized cubes. Place in boiling water and parboil 5 or 6 minutes, until the meat is cooked through. Drain and pat dry.

2. Slice garlic thinly. Cut chives into 1½-inch (4-cm) lengths.

3. Heat the oil in a fry pan, add livers, and sauté briefly over low heat. Place on a plate and set aside.

4. Discard some of the oil. In the same pan, sauté the garlic until fragrant. Return livers to the pan and stir-fry very briefly over high heat. Remove from heat and season with soy sauce and saké.

5. Return pan to the fire and add the chives. Sprinkle with ground pepper and stir-fry a few seconds over high heat. Remove from pan and serve immediately, before the chives turn watery.

Liver takes time to cook, which is why it's best to parboil it well before frying it over low heat. Add chives only at the very end, and stop cooking when they still look underdone.

CHINESE CHIVES

Crispy Fried Chicken

20 | Serves 4
263 cal/serving

3 boneless chicken thighs
1 tsp fresh ginger juice
2 Tbsp soy sauce
1 Tbsp saké
ground black pepper to taste

½ tsp sesame oil
3 to 4 heaping Tbsp potato starch
vegetable oil for deep-frying
a few sprigs of parsley

It is not necessary to use a lot of oil. If you fill a fry pan halfway with oil, the chicken pieces will be able to "air" during cooking, which makes them crispier.

1. Trim off excess fat and cut the chicken into bite-sized chunks. Season with ginger juice, soy sauce, saké, pepper, and sesame oil, and mix thoroughly. Coat chicken pieces with potato starch.

2. In a fry pan heat oil to medium (see page 19, note to "Breaded Shrimp"). Add chicken skin-side-down and fry until golden brown. Turn over.

3. Lower heat slightly, and continue frying until chicken is almost cooked. Return heat to high and turn chicken over once more, to crisp. Remove from oil and drain well.

4. Arrange on a serving plate and garnish with parsley.

To make ginger juice, grate the ginger and squeeze out the juice with your fingers. To make 1 teaspoon of juice, you will need a knob of fresh ginger about 1 inch (2½ cm) long.

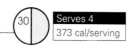

Minced Meat Cutlets

Serves 4
373 cal/serving

11 oz (300 g) ground pork and ground beef mixture (or all beef)

½ tsp salt

1 tsp Worcestershire sauce

½ onion

1 Tbsp vegetable oil + vegetable oil for deep-frying

2 to 3 cabbage leaves + cabbage leaves for garnish

1 bell pepper

flour

1 egg, beaten

breadcrumbs

mustard and Worcestershire sauce (optional)

1. Season the meat with salt and Worcestershire sauce and mix.

2. Chop the onion very fine and sauté in 1 tablespoon oil until transparent. Chop 2 to 3 cabbage leaves and the bell pepper very fine and mix thoroughly with the meat.

3. Divide the meat into 8 portions and shape into oval cutlets, with the middle indented a little.

4. Dip each cutlet into flour, egg, and breadcrumbs—in that order—and deep-fry over medium heat, (see page 19, note to "Breaded Shrimp"), until breadcrumbs turn golden-brown.

5. Remove from the oil and drain cutlets on a rack. Serve with a mound of cabbage leaves cut into thin strips and a dab of mustard. Drizzle with your favorite sauce.

Before shaping cutlets, toss them from one hand to the other to remove excess air. Then shape into patties that are longer and narrower than hamburgers.

Yakiniku Beef

Serves 4
275 cal/serving

2 generous Tbsp soy sauce

1 Tbsp roasted white sesame seeds

1 Tbsp sesame oil

1 clove garlic, grated

1 long green *naganegi* onion (or onion), finely chopped

ground black pepper to taste

14 oz (400 g) beef, loin or rump, thinly sliced

lettuce leaves

cherry tomatoes

In a wok, all the meat can be cooked at once, but a fry pan will also work fine if you cook meat in two or three batches. Or a tabletop griddle or barbecue makes it possible to cook as you eat.

1. Make the sauce in a large bowl by combining soy sauce, sesame seeds, sesame oil, garlic, long onion, and black pepper. Add the beef slices and mix thoroughly with the sauce.

2. Heat a wok until very hot and add the slices of beef, spreading them out so they do not overlap. Let the meat crisp on the bottom before briefly stir-frying it.

3. Arrange the meat in individual dishes over a bed of lettuce leaves, and garnish with cherry tomatoes. Serve immediately.

Since the sauce contains sesame oil, there is no need to use any oil for the stir-frying. A little oil can be used if desired.

Japanese-Style Hamburgers

30

Serves 4
416 cal/serving

14 oz (400 g) ground beef	1 egg	1 Tbsp saké
½ tsp salt	¼ cup milk	2 Tbsp Worcestershire sauce
ground black pepper to taste	1 cup breadcrumbs	1 tsp soy sauce
½ onion	⅔ cup water	1 Tbsp butter
vegetable oil for frying	3 Tbsp ketchup	

Toss the meat back and forth from one hand to the other to remove excess air. Then shape into patties.

1. Season the beef with salt and pepper and set aside.

2. Chop the onion very fine and sauté in a little oil until transparent. Remove from heat and set aside.

3. In a separate bowl, combine egg and milk and mix, then add breadcrumbs and mix briefly. Set aside to allow flavors to combine.

4. Add the onion mixture and the breadcrumb mixture to the beef. Mix lightly by squeezing the meat 2 or 3 times with your hands.

5. Dab a little oil on your palms and divide the meat into four portions. Toss each portion from one hand to the other, as if you were playing catch, to remove any excess air. Shape into 4 hamburgers, indenting the middle of each with your thumb.

6. Heat a little oil in a fry pan and sauté hamburgers over medium heat until nicely browned on one side. Turn and brown the other side.

7. Add enough boiling water to the pan to half-cover hamburgers. Cover the pan and simmer over medium-high heat until hamburgers are cooked through. Remove the lid, lower heat to medium, and continue cooking until all the liquid has evaporated. Place on individual plates and set aside.

8. To make the sauce, add water, ketchup, saké, Worcestershire sauce, soy sauce, and butter to the same pan, and bring to a boil. Simmer until slightly thickened and ladle the sauce over hamburgers. Serve with your favorite vegetables.

There are two secrets to making delicious hamburgers. First, prepare the breadcrumb mixture separately and mix into the beef very lightly, to make the meat light and fluffy. Second, be sure to add water to the fry pan, so the meat cooks through evenly.

Ginger Pork

15 | Serves 4
227 cal/serving

14 oz (400 g) pork, thinly sliced

2 Tbsp soy sauce

1 Tbsp *mirin* (or 1 Tbsp saké + 1 tsp sugar)

1 knob fresh ginger, grated

1 tsp sesame oil

vegetable oil for frying

cabbage leaves, roughly torn

1. Spread out two slices of pork and lay them one on top of the other. Lay out all the remaining slices this way.

2. In a bowl, make the sauce by combining soy sauce, mirin, grated ginger, and sesame oil.

3. Heat the vegetable oil in a fry pan. With chopsticks or a pair of tongs, pick up a pair of pork slices, quickly dip both sides into the sauce, and sauté over medium heat. When the meat changes color, turn it over and sauté until slices separate. Then sauté the uncooked sides so the meat is completely cooked. Continue to dip and sauté all the remaining slices.

4. Serve immediately on individual plates with fresh cabbage leaves.

Placing two slices of meat together before dipping them in sauce prevents the meat from absorbing too much seasoning.

Simmered Chicken Meatballs

20 | Serves 4
198 cal/serving

11 oz (300 g) ground chicken

1 tsp soy sauce + 2 Tbsp soy sauce

1 tsp saké + 2 Tbsp saké

½ tsp fresh ginger, grated

2 Tbsp potato starch

8 dried shiitake mushrooms

2 cups water

2 Tbsp *mirin* (or 2 Tbsp saké + 2 tsp sugar)

Use two spoons to scoop up a tablespoon of meat and slide it into the pan.

1. Season chicken with 1 teaspoon each of soy sauce and saké, grated ginger, and potato starch. Mix thoroughly.

2. Discard stems of shiitake mushrooms and cut mushrooms into halves or quarters. In a small pan, bring 2 cups of water to a boil, add mushrooms and simmer 4 to 5 minutes, until they swell.

3. Add 2 tablespoons saké, 2 tablespoons soy sauce, and mirin, and bring to a boil.

4. Make meatballs by scooping a tablespoon of ground chicken and sliding it into the pan. When all the meatballs are in the pan, cover, and simmer 10 or 15 minutes over medium heat until most of the liquid has evaporated. Shake the pan to coat meatballs evenly with sauce, and serve immediately.

Boiling dried shiitake mushrooms without reconstituting them first makes them chewy and delicious. The mushrooms absorb water and, at the same time, flavor the stock as they simmer.

These meatballs are eaten as they are, as a main dish. They go well with white rice and with side dishes of green vegetables like broccoli or spinach.

Stir-Fried Beef and Lettuce with *Kimchi*

10 | Serves 3–4
112 cal/serving

7 oz (200 g) beef, loin or rump, thinly sliced
½ cup *kimchi* spicy Korean pickled cabbage
½ head lettuce

1 Tbsp sesame oil
2 pinches of salt

The secret of stir-frying is not to stir the beef too much as it cooks. But once the meat changes color, stir-fry it briefly, to keep it from becoming watery. Serve quickly, before the lettuce wilts.

1. Cut beef into strips about 1½ inches (4 cm) long. Cut kimchi into bite-sized pieces. Mix beef and kimchi.

2. Tear lettuce leaves roughly into bite-sized pieces.

3. Heat the sesame oil in a wok until quite hot. Add beef and kimchi, and sauté over high heat until the meat turns color.

4. Add the lettuce, season with salt, and stir-fry briefly, until lettuce leaves just begin to wilt.

5. Remove from wok and serve immediately.

When the wok is very hot, spread the meat and kimchi evenly and allow them to cook undisturbed.

Sweet and Spicy Beef Curry

15 | Serves 4
264 cal/serving

ACTIVE TIME 15 min.
TOTAL TIME 35 min.

4 portions hot cooked rice
1 onion
1 carrot
1 clove garlic
1 knob fresh ginger
1 Tbsp vegetable oil for frying

5 cups water
1 pack curry roux (approx. 3½ oz/100 g)
11 oz (300 g) beef, thinly sliced
red *fukujin-zuke* pickles (or any pickles)
pickled *rakkyo* scallions (optional)

Curry roux is a dry curry paste sold in Asian markets in a form that looks like a larger chocolate bar.

1. Make the rice (see page 89). While rice is cooking, cut the onion into bite-sized pieces. Cut the carrot into ¾-inch (2-cm) half-rounds. Finely chop the garlic and ginger.

2. Heat the oil in a pan. Before it gets very hot, add the garlic and ginger, and sauté until fragrant. Add the onion and carrot, and sauté another minute or so.

3. Add the water, cover the pan, and simmer 10 minutes, until carrot becomes soft. Remove the pan from heat and add the curry roux, stirring until it is completely dissolved.

4. Return the pan to the fire and add the beef, one slice at a time, as this makes it more tender. Stir well and cook until heated through.

5. Serve with hot white rice and garnish with a little red pickles and pickled scallions.

Taking the pan off the fire lets the curry roux dissolve evenly.

Grated cheese also makes a good substitute for pickled onions.

Gyoza Pot Stickers

40 | **Serves 3–4**
| 302 cal/serving

Add more hot water to the fry pan if necessary.

4 leaves cabbage

1/2 bunch (2 oz/50 g) *nira* Chinese chives

1 clove garlic

1 Tbsp potato starch

5 1/2 oz (150 g) ground pork

1 Tbsp soy sauce

2 tsp sesame oil

2 tsp water

20 round *gyoza* wrappers

vegetable oil for frying

soy sauce, rice vinegar, and *rayu* Chinese hot chili oil to taste

1. Boil the cabbage and let it cool, then chop it very fine. Pick up a handful and squeeze out as much liquid as you can. Cut chives finely and chop the garlic. Combine cabbage, chives, and garlic, and mix in the potato starch with chopsticks or a fork.

2. Combine the pork, soy sauce, sesame oil, and water, and mix well. Add the cabbage mixture and mix thoroughly.

3. Place a teaspoonful of filling in the center of each wrapper. Moisten a finger and run it halfway around the inside edge of the wrapper. Fold one edge over to make a half-moon shape and squeeze the edges to seal.

4. Heat a fry pan until very hot. Add the oil, lower heat, and arrange the gyoza in the pan in rows. Fry lightly until the bottom turns golden brown. Add enough hot water to the pan to half-submerge the gyoza (the pan is liable to sizzle and steam, so have a lid handy), and cover the pan. Turn heat up to high, and steam until most of the liquid evaporates.

5. Remove the lid, lower heat, and cook until the pan is dry and gyoza are sizzling.

6. Scoop up gyoza with a spatula, place them upside-down on a serving plate, and serve immediately. Set out individual bowls for the dipping sauce, which each person can make to taste.

If you the mix the potato starch into the chopped vegetables with chopsticks or a fork, a film forms over the mixture that prevents it from getting watery (don't use your hands for this!).

Onion also works well as a substitute for Chinese chives.

A common ratio for the dipping sauce is equal parts vinegar and soy sauce, with a dash of rayu Chinese hot chili oil.

Variation: Boiled gyoza

1. Carefully slide gyoza into a pan of boiling water with 1 tablespoon of vegetable oil added. Cook over high heat about 10 minutes. Drain and arrange on a serving plate.

2. Garnish with chopped onion and ginger and set out individual bowls of dipping sauce.

Figure 1

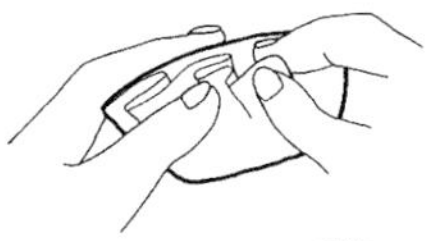

Figure 2

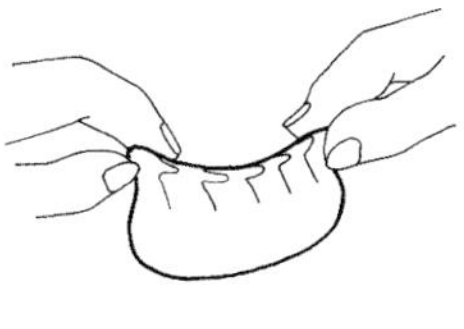

People usually make "tucks" in the back of the gyoza. If you are right-handed, hold the filled gyoza in your left hand and pull up the back edge toward the front. Start at one end and pull it up to the front edge while making small pleats in the back edge (Figure 1). When you are finished, squeeze all around the edges to secure the seal (Figure 2).

Steamed *Shumai* Dumplings

30

Serves 4
308 cal/serving

Making the onion mixture in a separate step, before adding the pork, makes the filling lighter.

½ onion
11 oz (300 g) ground pork
½ tsp salt
ground black pepper to taste
1 tsp sesame oil
3 heaping Tbsp potato starch

24 square *shumai* wrappers
hakusai Chinese cabbage leaf (or cabbage leaf)
soy sauce and rice vinegar to taste
mustard to taste

1. Chop the onion finely.

2. Season the pork with salt and pepper. Add the sesame oil and mix well with your hand, as though kneading dough. Set aside to allow time for the seasonings to blend.

3. Place the onion in a large bowl, add the potato starch, and mix with chopsticks or a fork. Add the pork mixture and mix well with your hand. Make individual shumai by placing a heaping teaspoonful of this mixture in the center of the wrapper and pulling the edges up around it like a pouch (Figure 1).

4. Spread a cabbage leaf on the bottom of a steamer (Figures 2 and 3) and arrange the shumai over it, taking care as much as possible that the shumai don't touch (since they will stick to one another).

5. Heat a good amount of water (at least 1 inch/2½ cm) in the pan. When it comes to a boil, place the steamer in or on the pan (depending on the type of steamer used) and cover the pan. Steam for 15 minutes over high heat.

6. Serve on a plate and set out small dishes for the dipping sauce of soy sauce, vinegar, and mustard. You can eat the cabbage too!

If you the mix the potato starch through the onion and pork with chopsticks or a fork, a film forms over the mixture and prevents it from getting watery (don't use your hands for this!).

Shumai can easily be reheated in the microwave (together with the cabbage leaf).

Use a large metal steamer with separate upper and lower compartments. Or, if you use a small folding metal steamer, place it in a large pot and set three or four small empty cans or ceramic cups on the bottom, to raise the steamer and allow more water to fit in the pan.

Figure 1

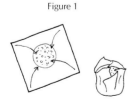

Figure 2

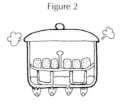

Figure 3

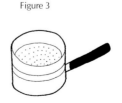

Cover the shumai with the cabbage leaf until ready to eat. This keeps them warm and prevents them from drying out.

Crunchy Daikon Salad

15 | Serves 4
172 cal/serving

6- to 7-inch (15- to18-cm) piece of daikon

4 slices bacon

½ tsp vegetable oil + 1 Tbsp vegetable oil

½ tsp salt

1 Tbsp rice vinegar

ground black pepper to taste

1 Tbsp lemon juice

daikon leaves to taste, chopped fine

Japanese *sansho* pepper (or *shichimi toga-rashi* red pepper) to taste

DAIKON

1. Peel the daikon and cut into several sections, each about 2 inches (5 cm) long. Cut into matchsticks and place in a large bowl of cold water for about 5 minutes to crisp. Drain well in a colander.

2. Cut the bacon into strips ¼ inch (5 mm) wide. Heat ½ teaspoon of oil in a fry pan and fry bacon over low heat until crispy. Drain on paper towels.

3. In a salad bowl, combine salt, vinegar, pepper, lemon juice, and 1 tablespoon oil—in that order—and mix well.

4. Add daikon, daikon leaves, and bacon, and toss.

5. Serve with a sprinkling of Japanese sansho pepper to enhance the flavor.

If you do not have daikon leaves, celery leaves will substitute.

45

Tomato Ginger Salad

10 | Serves 4
35 cal/serving

2 large ripe tomatoes
1 knob fresh ginger
2 Tbsp rice vinegar

2 Tbsp honey
2 pinches of salt
8 *shiso* perilla leaves

PERILLA LEAVES

1. Chill tomatoes, and cut into ½-inch (1½-cm) cubes. Peel the ginger, and cut into thin slivers along the grain and then into very fine slivers.

2. Make the dressing by combining vinegar, honey, and salt, and mixing well.

3. Line a plate with perilla leaves, and arrange tomatoes on top. Drizzle with the honey dressing, top with slivered ginger, and serve.

If perilla leaves are not available, substitute celery leaves or shredded lettuce.

Mushrooms Steamed in Saké

10 | Serves 4
12 cal/serving

6 to 8 fresh shiitake mushrooms
1 pack (3½ oz/100 g) *shimeji* mushrooms
1 pack (3½ oz/100 g) *enoki* mushrooms
salt to taste

2 Tbsp saké
2 Japanese *sudachi* limes (or 1 lemon)
soy sauce to taste

SHIMEJI MUSHROOMS

1. Remove stems of the shiitake mushrooms and the hard ends of the other mushroom stems. Cut shiitake caps into bite-sized pieces and separate the other mushrooms into small clusters.

2. Slightly wet a pan (to prevent sticking) and arrange mushrooms evenly in it. Season with salt and saké, cover the pan, and cook over high heat until steam spurts out from under the lid. Stir quickly, replace the lid, and heat a few more seconds.

3. Remove to a serving dish. Squeeze the juice of fresh Japanese limes over mushrooms and flavor lightly with soy sauce. Serve immediately.

All the different kinds of mushrooms go into the pot at the same time.

This recipe is also delicious with a combination of just shiitake and button mushrooms.

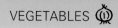

Crushed Cucumber Salad

10 | **Serves 4** / 64 cal/serving

ACTIVE TIME 10 min.
TOTAL TIME 30 min.

8 cucumbers, unpeeled
1 knob fresh ginger, unpeeled
¼ cup soy sauce

¼ cup saké
½ tsp *rayu* Chinese hot chili oil

Blanch cucumbers for a few seconds in small batches, and add them to the dressing.

1. Crush cucumbers by hitting them with a rolling pin or wooden pestle until they crack open. Then break them with your fingers into bite-sized lengths. Chop the ginger finely.

2. To make the dressing, combine soy sauce, saké, chili oil, and ginger in a large bowl and mix.

3. Bring a pan of water to a fast boil and add cucumbers in 2 or 3 batches. Blanch for a few seconds, scoop out with a slotted spoon, and drain.

4. Place cucumbers in the dressing for 20 minutes before serving. For a fuller flavor, refrigerate overnight.

Crushing the cucumbers gives them a jagged surface that allows flavor to penetrate better than if they were cut with a knife.

Blanched Spinach Salad

10 | **Serves 2–4** / 25 cal/serving

1 bunch spinach (10 oz/280 g)
½ tsp salt
1 Tbsp *dashi* stock (or water)

2 tsp soy sauce
dried *katsuobushi* bonito flakes to taste

1. Bring a pot of water to a boil, add the salt, and gently slide spinach in, leaves first. When completely immersed, turn over and blanch until stems are slightly soft, about 3 minutes.

2. Take the spinach from the water and immediately plunge it into a bowl of cold water. Change the water 3 or 4 times until it is no longer warm, and soak spinach for 5 minutes.

3. Remove spinach from the water, lay it neatly on a cutting board, and press down to remove water. Discard root parts, cut spinach into 1-inch (2½-cm) lengths, loosen a little, and arrange on a dish.

4. Mix dashi stock (see page 90) and soy sauce, and pour over the spinach. Sprinkle with dried bonito flakes.

Sliding the spinach in leaves first keeps the leaves immersed and allows the spinach to cook evenly.

Any leftovers can be kept in the refrigerator for several days, even if you have already added the dashi stock, soy sauce, and bonito flakes. In fact, if you sauté the leftovers in a little vegetable oil, with these seasonings added, the flavor becomes very rich.

Simmered Kabocha Squash

⏱ 15 | **Serves 4** / 71 cal/serving

¼ kabocha squash (8 oz/225 g)
  (or pumpkin)
1 to 1½ cups water
1 Tbsp *mirin* (or 1 Tbsp saké + 1 tsp sugar)

1 Tbsp sugar
1 Tbsp saké
1 Tbsp soy sauce

1. Remove pulp and seeds from the kabocha, peel skin here and there, and cut into 1-inch (2½-cm) cubes.

2. Moisten a pan (to prevent sticking) and place kabocha in it skin-side-down. Add enough water to more or less cover the kabocha (the tops should stick out a bit) and season with mirin, sugar, saké, and soy sauce. Cover the pan and bring to a boil over high heat. Lower heat to medium and simmer, still covered, for 10 minutes, or until a toothpick passes through easily. (If the water should evaporate before the kabocha becomes soft, add hot water—not cold—to the pan.)

3. Turn off heat and keep the pan covered for 5 minutes to steam before serving.

Kabocha are easier to cut if they are heated briefly beforehand. Place whole or cut in half in a pan of hot water and let it come to a fast boil. Or simply heat in a microwave 1 or 2 minutes.

Peeling the kabocha here and there allows flavors to penetrate better.

Cooking kabocha skin-side-down helps it keep its shape.

Asparagus Sauté

⏱ 10 | **Serves 4** / 67 cal/serving

7 to 8 asparagus spears
2 tsp vegetable oil

½ Tbsp soy sauce
a pinch of roasted white sesame seeds

1. Cut off the hard base of the asparagus spears. Peel the lower part of each spear and cut spears into 3 or 4 pieces of about equal length. Cut any thicker sections in half lengthwise.

2. Heat the oil in a fry pan and sauté asparagus over medium-high heat until cooked through.

3. Turn off heat briefly to add the soy sauce. Then sauté over medium heat, stirring constantly to keep asparagus from burning, until all the liquid evaporates.

4. Sprinkle with roasted sesame seeds and serve immediately.

Peel the lower part of each spear.

To roast, place in a fry pan and heat, shaking the pan constantly. When seeds turn golden brown, remove from heat. Roasted sesame seeds can also be ground slightly (this can be done between your fingers) to bring out the flavor.

Quick-Simmered Green Beans

15 | Serves 4
11 cal/serving

7 oz (200 g) green beans
1 bouillon cube

1½ cups water
ground black pepper to taste

1. String the beans, break each into 2 or 3 sections, and place in a pan.

2. Fill the pan with enough water to cover beans, add the bouillon cube, and cover the pan. Simmer beans over medium heat 5 to 10 minutes, until tender.

3. Remove to a serving dish and sprinkle with black pepper to taste.

Select beans that are bright green and on the slender side.

Bean Sprout Salad with Ground Pork

15 | Serves 2–4
84 cal/serving

1 pack (9 oz/250 g) bean sprouts
salt to taste
3½ oz (100 g) ground pork
1 Tbsp rice vinegar

1 Tbsp soy sauce
dash of sesame oil
1 Tbsp pickled red *benishoga* ginger, or fresh ginger, cut into fine slivers (optional)

BEAN SPROUTS

1. Bring a pan of lightly salted water to a boil. Add bean sprouts and blanch about 1 minute. Scoop out with a slotted spoon and place in a colander to cool.

2. In the same pan of boiling water, add the ground pork and boil until it turns color. Drain in a colander.

3. To make the dressing, combine vinegar, soy sauce, and sesame oil in a large bowl, and mix. Add the pork to the dressing and mix well.

4. When the pork cools, mix in bean sprouts in 2 or 3 batches, until all ingredients are thoroughly mixed.

5. Add pickled red ginger, stir once more, and serve.

Choose bean sprouts that are white and firm. If you see water in the pack, the sprouts are no longer fresh.

This dish is also good with alfalfa in place of bean sprouts.

Sweet Tomato Salad

Serves 3–4
48 cal/serving

3 to 4 ripe tomatoes
¼ onion
1 Tbsp rice vinegar

1 Tbsp honey
pinch of salt

If you do not have time to make this ahead, just soak whole tomatoes in ice water for a few minutes to cool instead.

1. Insert a fork into the caps of the tomatoes and plunge tomatoes in boiling water for 5 or 6 seconds, then immediately run cold water over them, and remove the skin. Discard the stem and cut tomatoes into thin wedges.

2. Chop the onion finely.

3. Make the dressing by combining vinegar and honey and stirring well.

4. Arrange tomatoes on a plate, place chopped onion on top, sprinkle with some salt, and drizzle dressing over. (If possible, make ahead and refrigerate for at least an hour, to allow flavors to blend.)

Blanching the tomato briefly makes it easy to remove the skin.

Simmered Shiitake Mushrooms

Serves 4
112 cal/serving

10 to 15 dried shiitake mushrooms
1 generous Tbsp sesame oil
1 Tbsp sugar
1 Tbsp *mirin* (or 1 Tbsp saké + 1 tsp sugar)

1 Tbsp soy sauce
1 Tbsp saké
1 cup mushroom water (or plain water)

DRIED SHIITAKE MUSHROOMS

Always reserve shiitake mushroom water, as it is an ideal flavor enhancer for simmered dishes or soups.

1. Reconstitute shiitake mushrooms by soaking them in warm water for a few minutes until they soften. Drain, reserving the mushroom water, and discard the stems.

2. Heat the sesame oil in a pan and briefly sauté mushrooms over medium heat. When mushrooms are heated through, turn off heat.

3. Add sugar, mirin, soy sauce, saké, and mushroom water, cover the pan, and simmer for about 10 minutes, or until most of the liquid evaporates. Serve immediately.

These mushrooms are a good accompaniment to Japanese Pan-Fried Chicken.

Cauliflower and Broccoli with Sesame Dip

10 | **Serves 4**
99 cal/serving

1 head cauliflower	1 Tbsp mayonnaise
1 head broccoli	1 Tbsp miso paste
1 Tbsp *shironeri goma* sesame paste	2 Tbsp milk

1. Separate the cauliflower and broccoli into florets. Remove the thick outer skin of the broccoli stem and cut the stem into 2-inch (5-cm) lengths.

2. In a pan of boiling water, add broccoli stems and cauliflower florets and blanch. Add broccoli florets and cook briefly. When vegetables are slightly tender, drain in a colander and spread in a single layer to cool.

3. Make the sesame dip by combining sesame paste, mayonnaise, miso paste, and milk in a small bowl, stirring vigorously until well blended.

4. Arrange cauliflower and broccoli on a large dish, with the bowl of sesame dip in the middle.

Broccoli stems and cauliflower florets are added to the boiling water first, and broccoli florets only after the water comes to a boil again.

Sesame dip is also great with uncooked vegetables.

Sesame paste is available in Asian markets. Or substitute Middle Eastern tahini, or any smooth, unsweetened nut butter, including peanut butter.

Eggplant and Peppers Sautéd in Miso

10 | **Serves 4**
49 cal/serving

6 to 8 small eggplants (each 3½ oz/100 g)	1 Tbsp saké
salt to taste	1 Tbsp soy sauce
2 small bell peppers	2 Tbsp sesame oil
1 Tbsp miso paste (red, if possible)	Japanese *sansho* pepper (or *shichimi togarashi* red pepper) to taste
1 Tbsp *mirin* (or 1 Tbsp saké + 1 tsp sugar)	

1. Discard stalk ends and cut each eggplant lengthwise in half, then cut on the diagonal into slices about ¼ inch (5 mm) wide. Place in cold water with some salt added (1 tablespoon salt to every 3 cups water) for 5 minutes, and pat dry with paper towels.

2. Remove caps and seeds from the peppers and cut lengthwise into slices about ¼ inch (5 mm) wide.

3. Combine miso paste, mirin, saké, and soy sauce in a bowl and set aside.

4. Heat the oil in a wok and stir-fry eggplants and peppers over high heat until eggplants become soft. Add the miso mixture, stir, and cook another minute or so.

5. Serve immediately, setting out Japanese pepper on the table.

Soaking eggplants in water before cooking prevents them from absorbing too much oil during stir-frying. Weight them down with a plate to keep them immersed.

The flavors of eggplant and miso complement each other very well.

Ginger Eggplant

Serves 4
137 cal/serving

6 to 8 small eggplants (each 3½ oz/
100 g)
salt to taste

1 knob fresh ginger, grated
2 Tbsp soy sauce
vegetable oil for frying

1. Discard eggplant caps and peel eggplants decoratively, in alternating strips (see photo). Cut each eggplant in half lengthwise and place in cold water with some salt added (1 tablespoon salt to every 3 cups water). Let stand 5 minutes and drain in a colander.

2. Mix grated ginger and soy sauce and place in a serving dish.

3. In a fry pan, heat the oil to medium (350°F/170° to 180°C). Pat eggplants dry with paper towels and sauté, skin-side-down, until they soften a little. Turn over and sauté the other side until a toothpick passes through easily. Remove from the pan and drain on a rack.

4. Place eggplants in the ginger and soy sauce dressing, and mix until evenly coated.

Choose eggplants that are firm and glossy and have sharp thorns on their caps.

Place the eggplants in the pan skin-side-down, as the skin side takes longer to cook. When they soften a little, turn over and sauté the other side.

Onion *Hitashi* Salad

Serves 4
28 cal/serving

1½ onions
a handful of *katsuobushi* dried bonito
flakes

soy sauce to taste
rice vinegar to taste

1. Cut onions in half down the center and slice thinly along the grain.

2. Bring a pan of water to a boil, add onions, and blanch until water begins to boil again. Drain immediately, spreading the onions in one layer to cool.

3. Place drained onions in a bowl, top with dried bonito flakes, and sprinkle with a little soy sauce and vinegar.

Slicing onions along the grain makes them crispier.

Simmered Mixed Vegetables

 40

Serves 4
368 cal/serving

8 small *satoimo* field yams
1 *gobo* burdock root
1 section *renkon* lotus root
1 block *konnyaku*
2 carrots
10 dried shiitake mushrooms
1 boiled bamboo shoot (5½ to 7 oz/150 to 200 g)

2 oz (50 g) snow peas
2 cups *dashi* stock
2 Tbsp light-colored (*usukuchi*) soy sauce
1 Tbsp soy sauce
1 Tbsp saké
1 to 2 Tbsp *mirin*

FIELD YAMS

1. Place field yams, washed but unpeeled, into a large pan of boiling water and boil 3 minutes over medium heat. Drain and peel.

2. Scrub the burdock root thoroughly to remove dirt and rinse well. Cut into 1-inch (2½-cm) lengths, and soak in a large bowl of water.

3. Peel the lotus root, cut into thin half-moons, and soak in another large bowl of water.

4. Cut the konnyaku thinly on the horizontal, as if you were cutting off pats of butter (Figure 1). "Knot" each slice of konnyaku by cutting a ¾-inch (2-cm) slit down the center (Figure 2), inserting one of the ends through it and pulling it straight (Figure 3).

5. Peel carrots and cut into ¼-inch (5-mm) rounds.

6. Reconstitute shiitake mushrooms by soaking them in warm water for 10 minutes until they soften. Drain and discard stems.

7. Cut the bamboo shoot into bite-sized pieces and rinse well.

8. Blanch snow peas briefly in lightly salted water.

9. Place yams, burdock root, lotus root, konnyaku, carrots, shiitake mushrooms, and bamboo shoot in a large pan. Add just enough water to cover vegetables, cover the pan, and boil over high heat until all the ingredients are cooked. Drain in a colander.

10. Return vegetables to the pan and add dashi stock, both kinds of soy sauce, and saké. Cover the pan and bring to a boil over high heat, then turn heat down to medium and simmer 15 minutes, until most of the liquid evaporates. (Shake the pan occasionally so vegetables will be evenly flavored.)

11. Add the mirin and bring to a boil again so that a nice glaze is formed.

12. Remove to a serving dish and decorate with snow peas.

If you like, chicken can be used in place of field yams. Cut 7 ounces (200 g) of meat into 1-inch (2½-cm) chunks.

Substitute 1 teaspoon regular soy sauce + ½ teaspoon salt for each tablespoon of light-colored soy sauce. For mirin, substitute 1 to 2 tablespoons saké + 1 to 2 teaspoons sugar.

Figure 1

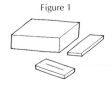

Figure 2

Figure 3

Omrice: Chicken Rice Omelette

Serves 4
418 cal/serving

ACTIVE TIME 30 min.
TOTAL TIME 65 min.

2 bell peppers

½ onion

1 chicken breast (5½ oz/150 g)

1 Tbsp vegetable oil + vegetable oil for frying

salt and ground black pepper to taste

4 generous Tbsp ketchup + 1 Tbsp ketchup for garnishing

4 portions hot cooked rice (each 4½ oz/130 g)

4 eggs

red *fukujin-zuke* pickles (or other pickles)

Boiling the chicken first removes excess fat and water. Reserve the stock for use in soups.

1. Cook the rice (see page 89).

2. When rice is cooked, remove caps and seeds from the peppers, and cut onion and peppers into ¼-inch (5-mm) cubes.

3. Trim off excess fat and cut the chicken into ¼-inch (5-mm) cubes. In a small pan of lightly salted boiling water, boil chicken until cooked through, drain, and set aside.

4. Heat the oil in a fry pan and sauté onion, peppers, and chicken over medium-high heat until vegetables are cooked. Season with salt and pepper and remove from heat.

5. Add the ketchup and return fry pan to the fire until the mixture begins to bubble. Turn off heat and add the rice. Mix briefly and set aside.

6. Make the omelettes one at a time. Beat 1 egg and season with salt. Heat the oil in a fry pan over medium heat and pour in the egg, letting it run evenly over the pan. When the egg is still slightly runny, place a quarter of the chicken rice in the center of the egg and fold the two ends over to make an omelette.

7. To remove the omelette, place a plate over the fry pan and turn the pan upside-down. Make the remaining omelettes in the same way. Drizzle with ketchup and garnish with pickles.

Briefly mixing the hot cooked rice with the chicken prevents the rice from tasting oily when it cools.

Add the chicken and rice before the egg is completely cooked. The omelette needs to be soft if it is to fold over.

Scrambled Eggs with Chinese Chives

10 | **Serves 4** | 85 cal/serving

1 bunch (3½ oz/100 g) *nira* Chinese chives
2 eggs
½ cup *dashi* stock

2 tsp light-colored (*usukuchi*) soy sauce
   (or 1 tsp soy sauce + ½ tsp salt)
1 Tbsp sesame oil

1. Discard the lower ends and cut chives into 1-inch (2½-cm) lengths.

2. Beat eggs lightly, without letting them become foamy. Season with dashi stock (see page 90) and soy sauce, add chives, and mix well.

3. Heat the oil in a wok over high heat and add the egg mixture, spreading it evenly over the surface. Cook quickly, stirring just once, when bubbles begin to form. (Eggs should be only lightly done.) Turn off heat and serve immediately.

Spread eggs and Chinese chives in the wok, and when mixture begins to bubble, gently turn over.

Eggs and Chinese chives go very well together. Chives should not be cooked too long or they will go limp and watery and will lose their flavor.

The secret is not to make this dish too salty—season only with dashi stock and soy sauce.

Crabmeat Omelette with Sweet-and-Sour Sauce

15 | **Serves 4** | 206 cal/serving

3½ oz (100 g) canned crabmeat
1 boiled bamboo shoot (3½ oz/100 g)
1 knob fresh ginger, peeled
6 eggs
salt to taste
saké to taste
1 cup water

1 Tbsp sugar
1 Tbsp light-colored (*usukuchi*) soy sauce (or 1 tsp regular soy sauce + ½ tsp salt)
1 Tbsp rice vinegar
1 Tbsp potato starch dissolved in 1 Tbsp water
4 tsp sesame oil

BAMBOO SHOOT

1. Flake the crabmeat and remove any bits of shell. Cut bamboo shoot and ginger into thin slices and then into matchsticks. Combine with the crabmeat and divide into 4 portions.

2. Moisten a bowl slightly with water (to prevent sticking), break the eggs in it, and season with salt and saké, and beat. Divide into 4 portions, each in a separate bowl. Place 1 portion of crabmeat mixture into each bowl of beaten egg.

3. Make the sweet-and-sour sauce by combining water, sugar, soy sauce, and vinegar in a small pan. Bring to a boil, add the dissolved potato starch, and stir until sauce thickens. Set aside.

4. In a wok, make 1 omelette at a time by heating 1 teaspoon of sesame oil over high heat, and adding 1 portion of the egg-and-crabmeat mixture. Stir quickly, with a few broad strokes, turn over, and briefly cook the other side. Remove to a plate and top with a little sweet-and-sour sauce. Make the remaining omelettes in the same way and serve immediately.

The omelettes are easier to make and taste better if you make them one at a time.

The trick is to get the wok very hot and cook the omelette quickly so that the egg stays runny inside.

Tofu with Sweet Miso Sauce

15

Serves 4
172 cal/serving

1 cake firm tofu

3 Tbsp miso paste (red, if possible)

3 Tbsp saké

1 Tbsp *mirin* (or honey)

1 Tbsp sugar

a small piece of Japanese *yuzu* citron peel
(or lemon peel, washed)

1 block *konnyaku*

½ Tbsp sesame oil

4 to 5 *shiso* perilla leaves, or lettuce or other
greens (optional)

Stir miso paste constantly with a wooden spoon, to keep it from burning.

If you don't have skewers, eat with chopsticks or with a knife and fork.

If shiso leaves are not available, lettuce or other greens can be substituted.

1. Place the tofu in a pan with just enough water to cover and bring to a boil over medium heat. Simmer 5 minutes, until the tofu is firm. Use a spatula to carefully remove it, and place it on a cutting board. Pat dry with paper towels.

2. Moisten a small pan with water (to prevent sticking), add miso paste, saké, mirin, and sugar, and bring to a boil over medium heat. When the mixture begins to bubble, turn heat to low and stir constantly with a wooden spoon until it becomes thick and glazed. Turn off heat and add a few gratings of citron peel.

3. Cut tofu and konnyaku into slices ¾ inch (2 cm) thick (working from one end, as if you were cutting off pats of butter). Make a series of crosshatches on one side of each konnyaku slice, to allow flavor to penetrate (Figure 1). If you have wooden skewers, insert a skewer through the center of each slice of tofu and konnyaku, to make it easy to pick up and eat.

Figure 1

4. Heat the oil in a fry pan and sauté tofu and konnyaku over medium-high heat until golden-brown on the outside and warm on the inside.

5. Spread a little miso mixture over each slice, and serve on a bed of perilla leaves.

Leftover miso mixture is delicious spread on toast!

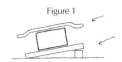

Golden Fried Tofu in Broth

Serves 4
181 cal/serving

2 cakes tofu (firm, if possible)

potato starch for dusting tofu + 1 Tbsp potato starch dissolved in 1 Tbsp water

all-purpose flour for dusting tofu

vegetable oil for deep-frying

1 Tbsp saké

1 Tbsp light-colored (*usukuchi*) soy sauce (or 1 tsp soy sauce + ½ tsp salt)

1 cup *dashi* stock

fresh ginger, grated (optional)

Figure 1

1. Place each cake of tofu on a cutting board and weight it with a plate (Figure 1). Tilt the board slightly, and leave for 15 minutes, to drain off excess liquid. Cut each cake in half to make 4 large squares.

2. Mix equal amounts of potato starch and flour, and coat tofu pieces thoroughly. Pat off any excess.

3. In a wok, heat oil to medium (see page 19, note to "Breaded Shrimp"), and gently slide in the tofu. Gradually turn up the heat and fry until the underside turns golden. Turn tofu over carefully with a spatula and fry the other side until golden. Remove from wok and drain on paper towels.

4. In a small pan, combine saké, soy sauce, and dashi stock (see page 90), and bring to a boil. Add the dissolved potato starch and cook only until the sauce thickens.

5. Arrange the tofu on individual dishes, spoon some sauce over, and top with a little grated ginger. Serve immediately.

Slide the tofu in, one piece at a time, with a spatula and wait patiently for it to turn golden.

Mabo-dofu Chili Tofu

Serves 4
294 cal/serving

2 to 3 cakes tofu (firm or soft)

1 long green *naganegi* onion

1 knob fresh ginger

1 clove garlic

½ bunch (2 oz/50 g) *nira* Chinese chives

1 Tbsp miso paste (red, if possible)

2 Tbsp soy sauce

2 Tbsp saké

½ tsp sugar

½ tsp *tobanjan* Chinese spicy miso-chili paste

½ tsp oyster sauce

1 Tbsp vegetable oil

5½ oz (150 g) ground pork

½ cup water

1 Tbsp potato starch dissolved in 1 Tbsp water

½ tsp sesame oil

Cooking the pork with the miso-chili sauce before adding the tofu brings out the full flavor of the pork.

1. Cut tofu into ¾-inch (2-cm) cubes. Place in a pan, add enough water to cover, and bring to a boil over high heat. Simmer 2 to 3 minutes and drain in a colander.

2. Chop long onion, ginger, and garlic, and cut chives into very small pieces.

3. Make the spicy sauce by combining red miso paste, soy sauce, saké, sugar, tobanjan miso-chili paste, and oyster sauce.

4. Heat the oil in a wok and before it gets very hot add long onion, ginger, and garlic, and sauté until fragrant. Add the pork, sauté very briefly, and add the sauce. Continue to sauté over medium heat, separating the ground meat with a spatula or a fork, until the meat changes color.

5. Turn heat to high, add tofu, and mix in. Add the water and cook until tofu is heated through.

6. Add the chives and stir a few times. Add the dissolved potato starch and stir until sauce thickens and glazes. Serve immediately, with a drizzle of sesame oil.

When the pork has absorbed the spicy sauce, add tofu and water and cook quickly over high heat.

Summer *Udon* Salad
with Lemon-Sesame Sauce

20 | Serves 3–4
368 cal/serving

3 to 4 lettuce leaves
1 cucumber
1 tomato
3 slices ham
4 to 5 *shiso* perilla leaves

4 portions dried *udon* noodles (each 3 oz/ 80 g)
4 lemon wedges
mentsuyu noodle stock
roasted white sesame seeds to taste

1. Tear lettuce leaves into bite-sized pieces. Cut the cucumber lengthwise in half, then slice thinly on the diagonal. Cut the tomato down the center and into thin slices. Cut ham slices across the center and into matchsticks. Cut perilla leaves lengthwise in half, then across into thin strips.

2. Bring a large pot of water to a boil, add noodles, and cook until *al dente*. Rinse immediately in cold water and drain in a colander. Arrange noodles in individual dishes, top with lettuce, cucumber, tomato, ham, and perilla leaves, and garnish with lemon wedges.

3. Prepare mentsuyu noodle stock (see page 90). Pour over the noodles and sprinkle with a pinch of sesame seeds, crushing the seeds a little with your fingers to release the flavor.

This dish makes an entire meal. It can be eaten with chopsticks, or with a fork and spoon.

Yakisoba Noodles with Seafood

15 | Serves 2
514 cal/serving

½ onion

1 knob fresh ginger

½ squid (or 6 oz/170 g crabmeat)

4 cabbage leaves

4½ to 5½ oz (130 to 150 g) octopus leg meat (or 6 oz/ 170 g clams)

3 to 4 boiled shrimp

1 Tbsp vegetable oil + 1 Tbsp vegetable

oil for frying

1 tsp salt

ground black pepper to taste

1 Tbsp saké

2 portions fresh *yakisoba* noodles (each 5½ oz/150 g)

aonori seaweed flakes, or *nori* seaweed (optional)

pickled red *benishoga* ginger (optional)

1. Slice the onion very finely. Cut the ginger into thin slivers about 1 inch (2½ cm) long.

2. Cut the squid into strips ½ inch (1½ cm) wide by 2 inches (5 cm) long. Separate squid legs.

3. Cut cabbage leaves into bite-sized pieces. Cut octopus into rounds or into bite-sized pieces. Cut shrimp in half on the diagonal.

4. Heat 1 tablespoon of oil in a fry pan or wok and sauté onion and ginger until well coated with oil. Over high heat, briefly sauté each ingredient before adding the next, in the following order—squid, cabbage, octopus, and shrimp. Continue to sauté until all ingredients are cooked through. Season with salt, pepper, and saké, remove from wok, and set aside.

5. Heat the remaining tablespoon of oil in the same wok. Stir-fry noodles according to the instructions on the package. When noodles are done, return cooked ingredients to wok and stir-fry briefly over high heat, mixing well.

6. Sprinkle with aonori seaweed flakes or with a sprinkling of crumpled or shredded nori, and garnish with pickled red ginger.

If fresh yakisoba noodles are not available, substitute 2 portions dried spaghetti or beefun (thin rice noodles used in Chinese and Southeast Asian cooking), boiled until *al dente.*

Chilled Chinese Noodles

15 | **Serves 4**
460 cal/serving

1 bag bean sprouts (9 oz/250 g)

2 eggs

salt to taste

vegetable oil for frying

2 cucumbers

6 slices ham

6 Tbsp rice vinegar

5 Tbsp soy sauce

2 Tbsp sugar

1 tsp sesame oil

4 portions fresh *chukamen* Chinese egg
  noodles, each 4½ oz/130 g (or angel hair
  pasta)

pickled red *benishoga* ginger (optional; or
  regular fresh ginger, cut into very thin slivers)

mustard (optional)

roasted white sesame seeds (optional)

The eggs are prepared this way in Japan, but it's also fine to just scramble 2 eggs, and use them in place of the thin sheets of egg.

Remove the thin sheet of egg and lay it on top of the other sheets.

This dish can be eaten with chopsticks or with a fork and soup spoon.

1. Blanch bean sprouts briefly in lightly salted boiling water, until slightly soft. Drain immediately and set aside to cool.

2. Beat eggs and season with salt. Heat the oil in a large fry pan and cook a quarter of the egg over medium-high heat, spreading it as thinly as possible over the whole pan. Remove the thin sheet of egg and fold in half on a cutting board. Cook the rest of the egg the same way and place the folded sheets one on top of another. Cut all into very thin strips.

3. Slice cucumbers thinly on the diagonal, then cut into matchsticks. Cut ham across the middle and into thin strips.

4. Make the sauce by combining vinegar, soy sauce, sugar, and sesame oil.

5. Bring a large pan of water to a fast boil, add noodles, and cook according to the instructions on the packet. Drain and rinse several times in cold water. Use ice water for the last rinsing, so noodles are completely chilled.

6. Serve noodles on individual plates, topped with bean sprouts, egg, cucumber, and ham. Sprinkle with pickled red ginger and sesame seeds, and place a dab of mustard at the edge of the plate. Finally, pour a quarter of the sauce over each serving.

Beef Bowl

10 | **Serves 4**
484 cal/serving

ACTIVE TIME 10 min.

TOTAL TIME 35 min.

Figure 1

4 portions hot cooked rice (each 4½ oz/130 g)

1 onion

1 to 2 long green *naganegi* onions

4 Tbsp soy sauce

2 Tbsp sugar

1 Tbsp saké

11 oz (300 g) beef, thinly sliced

pickled red *benishoga* ginger (optional)

Using two kinds of onions makes this dish especially delicious.

1. Make rice (see page 89). While rice is cooking, cut the onion in half down the middle and slice thinly along the grain. Cut long onions on the diagonal into slices ¼ inch (5 mm) wide (Figure 1).

2. In a shallow pan, combine onion, long onions, soy sauce, sugar, and saké, and bring to a boil over medium heat.

3. Turn heat to high and add the beef, a slice at a time, spreading out the slices in the pan. When all the beef is cooked, remove from heat and set aside.

Be careful not to overcook the beef. Also make sure the rice is hot, so that it will absorb the full flavor of the beef and sauce.

4. Divide the rice among four large bowls and top each with a quarter of the beef and onions and a little sauce. Garnish with a little pickled red ginger and serve.

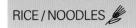

Oyakodon Chicken-and-Egg Rice

10 | Serves 4 | 433 cal/serving

ACTIVE TIME 10 min.
TOTAL TIME 35 min.

4 portions hot cooked rice (each 4½ oz/ 130 g)

7 oz (200 g) chicken

1 long green *naganegi* onion

2 cups *dashi* stock

3 Tbsp *mirin* (or 3 Tbsp saké + 1 Tbsp sugar)

3 Tbsp soy sauce

4 eggs

nori seaweed (optional)

Thin slices of onion can be substituted for the long green onion.

1. Make the rice (see page 89.) While rice is cooking, trim off excess fat from the chicken and cut the chicken into bite-sized pieces. Slice the long onion thinly on the diagonal.

2. In a shallow pan combine dashi stock (see page 90), mirin, and soy sauce, and bring to a boil. Add chicken and bring to a boil again over high heat. Add the long onion and cook 3 to 4 minutes, until the onion is tender and the chicken is cooked.

3. Beat eggs and pour them gently into the stock in a circular motion, taking care to cover chicken evenly. Cover the pan and cook 1 to 2 minutes over low heat. When eggs are just set but still runny, turn off heat and allow pan to steam, covered, a minute or so.

4. Divide the rice among 4 deep bowls and spread a quarter of the chicken-and-egg mixture over each. Serve hot with a sprinkling of torn or shredded nori.

The secret is to add the beaten egg when there's still stock left in the pan and to avoid cooking it too long.

This dish is called "Mother-and-Child Rice Bowl" in Japanese, since it features both chicken and egg.

Mushroom Rice

10 | Serves 4 | 310 cal/serving

ACTIVE TIME 10 min.
TOTAL TIME 35 min.

2 cups uncooked rice

2²/₅ cups water

1 pack *shimeji* mushrooms (3½ oz/100 g)

1 pack fresh shiitake mushrooms (3½ oz/ 100 g)

½ sheet deep-fried *abura-age* tofu

2 Tbsp saké

½ tsp salt

1 Tbsp soy sauce

Japanese *yuzu* citron peel (optional)

YUZU CITRON

1. Wash the rice at least 15 minutes before you are ready to cook it. Add the water, remove 3 tablespoons of water from it, and set rice aside to soak.

2. Trim off the hard ends of the shimeji mushroom stems and separate into small clusters. Trim the shiitake mushroom stems, then cut the caps into thin strips and the stems vertically.

3. Hold the deep-fried tofu under hot running water to remove excess oil, and squeeze out the water. Cut down the middle and into thin strips.

4. Combine saké, salt, and soy sauce, add to the uncooked rice, and stir. Arrange mushrooms and deep-fried tofu evenly over the rice, and cook the rice (see page 89). Let it steam 10 minutes after cooking.

5. Gently mix the cooked rice with a damp rice paddle or wooden spoon so that the ingredients are evenly distributed. Serve in individual bowls garnished with a little grated citron peel.

If you prefer, you can substitute chicken for the deep-fried tofu. Use 3½ ounces (100 g) of thigh or leg meat, cut up small. Add to the rice without cooking it first.

This dish goes well with hearty soups like Assorted Vegetable Soup, or with such vegetables as spinach or kabocha squash.

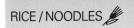

Toasted *Onigiri* Rice Balls

Serves 4
465 cal/serving

ACTIVE TIME 30 min.
TOTAL TIME 65 min.

cooked rice for 8 to 12 *onigiri* rice balls
   (each 4½ oz/130 g)
soy sauce to taste

miso paste to taste
saké (or *mirin*)

Put enough rice to make one rice ball into a small bowl before handling, to help cool it off.

1. Cook the rice (see page 89). When cooked, remove the lid, to let the rice cool down a little.

2. Moisten a small rice bowl (or coffee cup) with water and put a handful of cooked rice into it loosely, using a damp rice paddle or wooden spoon.

3. Moisten the palms of your hands, shake off any excess water, and rub a little salt onto your palms. Empty the rice from the small bowl onto one palm (if you are right-handed, the left palm).

4. Press the rice between your palms to give it the basic ball shape. Then turn the ball of rice so that it is sitting in your palm on one edge, and continue turning it, pressing down lightly on each edge as you do so, to give it a triangular shape.

5. Heat the oven or toaster oven to 400°F (200°C), place the rice balls lying down on the rack, and bake or toast 20 minutes.

6. Dilute some miso paste with a little saké or mirin.

7. When rice balls first begin to take on a golden color, remove them from the oven. Spread the miso mixture very thinly over both sides of half the rice balls. Use a brush to baste the others with soy sauce.

8. Return to the oven, and bake another 5 to 10 minutes. (If the color is still not rich enough, baste the soy sauce rice balls again.)

Moisten your palms slightly and rub some salt on them.

Press rice between your palms to give it the basic ball shape.

Spread the miso mixture thinly over both sides of the rice ball.

In the photo on the opposite page, soy sauce rice balls are shown on the left, and miso rice balls on the right.

Oyster Rice

10 | Serves 4
408 cal/serving

ACTIVE TIME 10 min.
TOTAL TIME 35 min.

2 cups uncooked rice

2²/₅ cups water

11 oz (300 g) small oysters, shucked

1 knob fresh ginger

yuzu Japanese citron peel (optional)

2 Tbsp saké

1 Tbsp soy sauce

½ tsp salt

1 tsp *mirin* (or 2 pinches of sugar)

1. Wash the rice at least 15 minutes before you are ready to cook it. Add the water, remove 3 tablespoons of water from it, and set rice aside to soak.

2. Rinse oysters well by placing them in a bowl of cold water, rinsing them a few times, and discarding the water. Repeat this process several times and drain well. Cut any larger oysters in half.

3. Peel the ginger and cut into thin slices and then into matchsticks. Cut the citron peel into very thin shavings.

4. Combine saké, soy sauce, salt, and mirin, and add to the rice. Then arrange oysters and ginger strips evenly over the rice and cook (see page 89). Let the rice steam 10 minutes after cooking.

5. Gently mix the rice with a damp rice paddle or wooden spoon so that the ingredients are evenly distributed throughout. Serve in individual bowls, garnished with a little citron peel.

Arrange oysters and ginger strips evenly over the rice. The secret ingredient in this dish is the fresh ginger.

This dish goes well with spinach or green beans, and with Miso Soup with Tofu and Nameko Mushrooms.

Miso Soup with
Short-Necked Clams

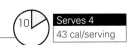

10 | Serves 4
43 cal/serving

6 oz (170 g) fresh *asari* short-necked clams
3½ cups water

2 to 3 Tbsp miso paste
ground black pepper to taste

1. Place clams in a large bowl of cold water and remove any dirt with your fingers. Discard the water.

2. Place clams in a small pan, add 3½ cups water, and bring to a boil over high heat until all the clams are completely open.

3. Remove a little stock from the pan, dissolve the miso paste in it, and stir this into the stock. Turn off heat soon after the soup comes to a boil.

4. Serve in individual bowls with a little ground black pepper.

Clams have so much flavor that it is not necessary to use any dashi stock in this soup.

If you buy your clams from a fish market, they may need to be cleaned quite thoroughly. Soak in water slightly less salty than seawater before doing Step 1.

Miso Soup with
Wakame Seaweed

10 | Serves 4
28 cal/serving

When wakame is reconstituted, it doubles in size.

¼ cup dried *wakame* seaweed
4-inch (10-cm) section long green *naganegi* onion

4 cups *dashi* stock
2 to 2½ Tbsp miso paste

1. Reconstitute wakame seaweed by soaking in cold water for 3 to 6 minutes, or until soft. Squeeze out excess water and cut into 1-inch (2-cm) lengths. Cut the long onion into very thin slices.

2. Place dashi stock (see page 90) in a pan and bring to a boil over high heat. Add the seaweed, turn heat down to medium, and let it heat until the seaweed expands.

3. Remove a bit of soup from the pan, dissolve the miso paste in it, and stir this into the stock. Add the long onion and turn off heat soon after the soup comes to a boil. Serve immediately.

Do not cook wakame seaweed for more than a few seconds, as it tends to dissolve.

For additional flavor, add thin strips of deep-fried abura-age tofu.

Pork and Vegetable Soup

Serves 4
139 cal/serving

4-inch (10-cm) section *gobo* burdock root

2-inch (5-cm) piece carrot

2-inch (5-cm) piece daikon

1 small pack *shirataki* (*konnyaku* noodle strands; optional)

1 potato

2 *hakusai* Chinese cabbage leaves (or cabbage leaves)

½ Tbsp sesame oil

5½ oz (150 g) pork, thinly sliced

4 cups *dashi* stock

2 to 3 Tbsp miso paste

long green *naganegi* onion, chopped (or *wakegi* spring onion)

ground black pepper to taste

1. Scrub the burdock root thoroughly to remove dirt and rinse well. With a potato peeler, cut thin shavings of burdock into a large bowl of cold water. Soak peelings 4 or 5 minutes, and then drain well in a colander. Peel the carrot and cut into thin rectangular blocks. Peel the daikon and cut into thin rectangular blocks.

2. Rinse the shirataki and drain, then cut into easy-to-manage lengths. Cut the potato into bite-sized pieces. Cut stems of the Chinese cabbage lengthwise into 2-inch (5-cm) pieces and then into thin strips, and cut up leaves roughly.

3. Heat the sesame oil in a large pan and stir-fry pork and burdock root over high heat until the pork turns white. Add carrot, daikon, shirataki, potato, and cabbage—one at a time and in that order—and stir-fry each ingredient until well coated with oil.

4. Add the dashi stock (see page 90) and simmer over high heat until it comes to a boil. Turn heat down to medium and continue to cook until vegetables become soft.

5. Remove a little soup from the pan, dissolve the miso paste in it, and stir this into the stock. Soon after the soup begins to bubble, turn off heat.

6. Serve in individual bowls with a sprinkling of chopped long green onion and some pepper.

This soup is as hearty as a stew and goes well with either rice or bread.

Mushrooms, shiitake, bell peppers, or eggplants can be used in place of any of the vegetables here (just cut into similar sizes and stir-fry with the pork). Also ½ block of tofu can be substituted for the daikon.

Miso Soup with Tofu and *Nameko* Mushrooms

Serves 4
55 cal/serving

½ cake tofu

1 pack (3 oz/100 g) *nameko* mushrooms

4 cups *dashi* stock

2 Tbsp miso paste

a few stalks *mitsuba* trefoil (optional)

TREFOIL

1. Cut the tofu into bite-sized cubes. Rinse nameko mushrooms by placing them in a colander and running cold water over them.

2. Place the dashi stock (see page 90) in a pan, add mushrooms, and bring to a boil over high heat, then turn heat down to low.

3. Remove a little soup from the pan, dissolve the miso paste in it, and stir this into the stock. Add the tofu, heat through, and turn off heat soon after the soup comes to a boil.

4. Serve in individual bowls garnished with a little trefoil chopped into 1-inch (2½-cm) lengths.

Be sure to add the tofu after mixing in the miso paste. The tofu only needs to be heated through.

If trefoil is not available, try using snow peas cut into bite-sized pieces.

Assorted Vegetable Soup

Serves 4
175 cal/serving

20

1½-inch (4-cm) piece carrot

1½-inch (4-cm) piece daikon

1 block *konnyaku* (optional)

1 cake tofu

1 sheet deep-fried *abura-age* tofu

4 *satoimo* field yams (or 2 medium-sized potatoes)

1 long green *naganegi* onion (or chives)

1 pack (3½ oz/100 g) *shimeji* mushrooms (or button mushrooms)

1 Tbsp sesame oil

5 to 6 cups *dashi* stock

salt to taste

1 Tbsp saké

a dash of soy sauce

1 Tbsp potato starch dissolved in 1 Tbsp water

½ thin green *bannonegi* onion, chopped (or chives)

1 knob fresh ginger, grated

1. Cut carrot and daikon into ¼-inch (5-mm) rounds and then into quarters. Cut the konnyaku into bite-sized chunks. Cut the tofu in half lengthwise and then into strips ¾ inch (2 cm) thick. Cut the deep-fried tofu in half lengthwise and then into short, thin strips.

2. Peel field yams and cut into ¼-inch (5-mm) rounds. Cut the long onion into ¾-inch (2-cm) lengths. Discard hard ends of the mushroom stems and separate into small clusters.

3. Heat the oil in a fry pan and add carrot, daikon, konnyaku, tofu, and abura-age—one at a time and in that order. Sauté each ingredient over high heat until well coated with oil.

4. Add the dashi stock (see page 90) and bring to a boil. Add field yams, cover the pan, and simmer over low to medium heat until yams soften.

5. Add the long onion and mushrooms and season with salt, saké, and soy sauce. Stir in the dissolved potato starch, and turn off heat soon after the soup comes to a boil. Serve with chopped green onion and a little grated ginger.

Japanese-Style Egg-Drop Soup

Serves 4
73 cal/serving

10

4 cups *dashi* stock

½ tsp salt

1 Tbsp saké

1 tsp soy sauce

1 Tbsp potato starch dissolved in 1 Tbsp water

1 to 2 eggs, beaten

1 knob fresh ginger, grated (optional)

thin green *bannonegi* onion, finely chopped (optional)

When the soup thickens, slowly pour in the egg, with a circular motion.

1. Place the dashi stock (see page 90) in a small pan and season with salt, saké, and soy sauce. (For a stronger flavor, add more salt or soy sauce.) Bring to a boil.

2. Add the dissolved potato starch and stir until the soup thickens.

3. When the soup comes to a boil again, add the beaten egg by drizzling into the pan in a thin stream, moving your hand in a circular motion. As soon as the cooked egg floats up to the surface, cover the pan and turn off heat. Let stand 1 to 2 minutes.

4. Serve in individual bowls, with a little grated ginger and chopped green onion.

Be careful not to add too much potato starch. The soup should not be too thick.

Chives can be substituted for the green onion.

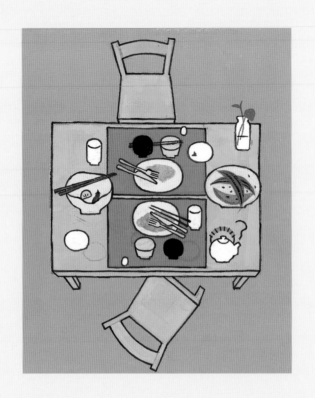

Basic Techniques

MAKING RICE

Serves 4 35 minutes

2 cups short- or medium-grain rice
2²⁄₅ cups water

1. Place rice grains in the detachable container of an automatic rice cooker or in a large pot. To wash rice, add twice the amount of water to the pot, rinse with your hand until the water becomes clouded, and push on the rice grains with the heel of your hand in a kneading motion (Figure 1). Drain and change the water, and repeat 3 or 4 times, until the water is clear.

2. Drain rice grains well, add the 2²⁄₅ cups water, and let rice soak for at least 15 minutes before cooking.

3. If using an automatic rice cooker, turn it on to cook the rice. If using a pot, cover the pot tightly, and bring to a boil over high heat. When the pot starts to steam and the lid begins to shake, turn heat down to low. (If the pot seems about to boil over, move the lid off slightly; Figure 2.)

4. Cook another 10 minutes, until all the water has been absorbed, then turn off heat. (If you moved lid off earlier, replace it, so that the rice can steam properly.)

5. Let the rice steam, off the heat, for 10 minutes.

The ratio of rice to water should be 1 to 1.2.

Figure 1

Figure 2

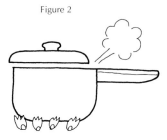

MAKING *DASHI* STOCK

5 minutes

4 to 5 cups water

a handful of dried *katsuobushi* bonito
flakes

This keeps well in the refrigerator for about 2 days, or in the freezer for a week to 10 days.

1. Bring the water to a boil, add bonito flakes, and turn heat down to low. Simmer on low for about 1 minute, then turn off heat.

2. Remove from heat and pour contents of the pan through a sieve into a bowl. With the back of a soup ladle, press against the sieve to squeeze out all the the flavor.

Squeeze with the back of a soup ladle or spoon.

MAKING *MENTSUYU* NOODLE STOCK

ACTIVE: 10
TOTAL: 25

4 cups water

4-inch (10-cm) piece of dried *konbu* kelp

2 handfuls of dried *katsuobushi* bonito
flakes

⅓ cup *mirin* (or 4 Tbsp saké + 1 Tbsp sugar)

⅓ cup light-colored (*usukuchi*) soy sauce
(or 1½ Tbsp regular soy sauce + 2 tsp salt)

1 Tbsp saké

This stock will keep in the refrigerator for 3 or 4 days, and longer in the freezer.

Noodle stock is also available bottled, in Asian markets.

1. Rinse kelp very briefly under running water and place in a large pan. Add the water and let sit for at least 15 minutes (if you have time, soak 30 minutes or more).

2. Add bonito flakes, mirin, and light-colored soy sauce. Bring to a boil over high heat, and then turn heat down to low and simmer 2 or 3 minutes. Remove from heat and pour contents of the pan through a sieve into a bowl. With the back of a soup ladle, press against the sieve to squeeze out the last bits of flavor.

Let kelp soak for 30 minutes or more.

Add the katsuobushi.

Add the mirin, light-colored soy sauce, and saké.

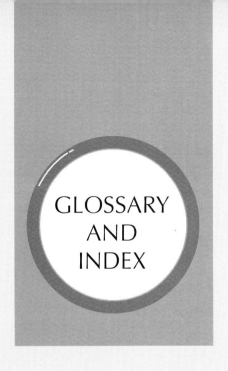

GLOSSARY
AND
INDEX

Glossary

abura-age
See tofu.

aonori seaweed flakes
See nori.

bamboo shoots (*takenoko*)
Readily available in grocery stores or Asian markets. Blanch canned shoots briefly before using, to get rid of any slight metallic taste. Store leftover shoots in water in the refrigerator up to 1 week, changing the water every day.

bannōnegi (thin green onions)
Sometimes available fresh in Asian markets. Chives or chervil will always substitute.

beefun (thin rice noodles)
Available dried in Asian markets, these need to be soaked until soft, about 15 minutes, before use.

benishōga (pickled red ginger)
See ginger.

bonito flakes
See katsuobushi.

burdock root (*gobō*)
This root is a good source of dietary fiber and nutrients. Much of the flavor is near the skin, so burdock should always be scrubbed rather than peeled. After shaving the root into thin peels, these should be immersed in cold water to remove any astringency.

Chinese cabbage (*hakusai*)
Also known as bok choy. Available fresh in Asian markets and most supermarkets.

Chinese chives (*nira*)
These look like flatter chives, and have a delicate, garlicky flavor.

Chinese spicy miso-chili paste (*tōbanjan*)
This paste of fermented beans infused with mashed chili peppers, vinegar, and other seasonings is available in small glass jars in Asian markets. It has a distinctive flavor and gives a bright red color to various dishes that are Chinese in origin.

chūkamen (Chinese noodles)
Egg noodles used in Chinese-style dishes such as the well-known dish ramen. *Chūkamen* should be available fresh (in vacuum-sealed packs in the refrigerator section) or dried in Asian markets.

curry roux
Prepared curry paste sold in Asian markets in a form that resembles a chocolate bar. It comes in three varieties: mild, medium hot, and hot.

daikon (giant white radish/Japanese radish/Chinese radish)
This is eaten in many ways—one of which is grated and served as a condiment, with a drizzle of soy sauce. It is served this way with tempura and grilled fish for the tangy flavor it gives and its ability to aid in the digestion of oily foods. It is available fresh in Asian markets and is a good source of vitamin C. Small Western red radishes can not be substituted for daikon, although Chinese or Western white radishes can.

dashi (fish-based soup stock)
Dashi is a stock flavored with flakes of bonito and then strained. This stock is used not only in soups but also as the flavor base for many simmered dishes. A bottled version is also available in Asian markets.

enoki mushrooms
These tiny white mushrooms are mild in flavor and high in fiber. They have slender stems 2 to 3 inches (1 cm) long and very small caps. The mushrooms are connected at the hard base, which needs to be cut away. Available fresh at some Asian markets. Other kinds of mushrooms, including button mushrooms, will substitute.

field yams (*satoimo*)
Also known as taro, these are sometimes available fresh in Asian markets. *Satoimo* are a kind of sticky potato with a hairy peel and should be scrubbed well before use. Potatoes will substitute.

fukujin-zuke
Red *fukujin-zuke* ("seven lucky god pickles") are invariably used to accompany Japanese-style curry and rice. They consist of a mixture of 7 vegetables sliced thin and pickled in soy sauce and *mirin*. May

be available in small jars in Asian markets. Any pickle will substitute.

ginger (*shōga*)

Fresh ginger is knobby and a golden beige color. Sold in Asian markets and many supermarkets. As a substitute, avoid powdered ginger, which is not nearly as pungent, and instead use the paste that is available in tubes or jars.

Benishōga is a form of ginger that is red-tinted and pickled in vinegar. Used as a condiment, it is usually available in the refrigerator case in Asian markets. Fresh ginger will also substitute.

gobō

See burdock root.

gyōza wrappers

Thin circles of dough made from wheat flour, eggs, and water. Sold in 1-pound plastic-wrapped packages of 80 to 100 skins and available in the refrigerator case in Asian markets. Wonton wrappers are thinner, but can substitute if necessary.

kabocha (Japanese squash/Japanese pumpkin)

This variety is small for a pumpkin, usually no more than 8 inches (20 cm) in diameter, and has a greenish skin (the skin too is edible); the flesh inside is yellow-orange. Kabocha is prepared in many different ways. It is available in Asian markets and some supermarkets.

katakuriko

See potato starch

katsuobushi

Also known as *kezuribushi* and *hanagatsuo*, these shavings of dried bonito are used as a flavoring for *dashi* soup stock and in many other dishes, and often as a garnish. Packaged dried bonito flakes are widely available in Asian markets, sold in cellophane bags that come in a variety of sizes.

kelp (*konbu* seaweed)

This dried seaweed is sold in long, dark, leathery strands. Rich in minerals, it is used as a flavoring for soups and simmered dishes. It is not necessary to wipe off the white residue that often appears on the surface, although some cooks do. Will keep indefi-

nitely if stored in an airtight container. Available in natural food stores and Asian markets.

kimchi

This mainstay of Korean cooking is a very spicy pickled mixture of Chinese cabbage with salt, garlic, and red chili powder. Available in glass jars or cellophane bags in the refrigerator case in Asian markets and some supermarkets.

konbu

See kelp.

konnyaku (devil's tongue jelly/yam cake/konjac)

Sold in greyish-brown blocks packed in water in the refrigerator case of Asian markets; look for it near the tofu. A gelatinous paste made from the starchy roots of a plant known as devil's tongue, *konnyaku* has no calories and little taste; it is enjoyed mainly for its chewy texture. *See also shirataki.*

lotus root (*renkon*)

Available fresh in many Asian markets, this is a thick, whitish-gray root. Slicing it crosswise reveals an attractive flower pattern of air holes that run the length of the root. Boiled and sliced lotus is also available in cans.

mentsuyu (noodle broth)

Flavored with kelp, bonito flakes, *mirin*, and soy sauce, *mentsuyu* serves as the broth for many noodle dishes. A bottled version is available in Asian markets.

mirin

Golden sweet saké used only for cooking. It is available in some supermarkets and all Asian markets. Saké sweetened with sugar to taste will substitute, as will honey.

miso (fermented soybean) paste

A mainstay of Japanese cooking, this fermented paste of soybeans and barley, wheat, or rice is readily available in natural food stores and Asian markets. Highly nutritious, it is a good source of protein. It comes in many varieties, thicknesses, and colors; these are grouped into large categories of red and pale-colored miso. For the recipes in this book, either of these types can be used.

mitsuba
See trefoil.

mortar and pestle (*suribachi*)
The Japanese-style mortar is a deep bowl, the inside of which is ribbed and scored with many tiny grooves that act as a grater. It is usually available at Asian markets. A mini-food processor or spice grinder can be used instead.

naganegi (long green onions)
A long variety of welsh onion, it is used more as a condiment than as a vegetable. Similar to the leek, but thinner and much longer. Onions, chives or chervil can substitute. Despite the name, it is the white stem that is usually used.

nameko mushrooms
These small mushrooms have golden-brown caps on pale, short stems and are slippery in texture. They are available in Asian markets in small and medium-sized cans. Drain off the water-packing before use.

nira
See Chinese chives.

noodles
See *chūkamen*, *udon*, and *yakisoba*.

nori seaweed (laver)
These dried paper-thin sheets—black with just a hint of dark green—can be torn, crumpled, or cut with scissors. Will keep indefinitely if stored in an airtight container.

Brighter green *aonori* flakes (actually a different type of *nori*) are also available in small spice jars.

onion
See bannōnegi, naganegi.

perilla leaves (*shiso*)
A Japanese herb used fresh for seasoning and garnishing. Sold in the refrigerator section of Asian markets, and recognizable by their vivid green color and slightly serrated edges.

potato starch (*katakuriko*)
Used in many dishes as a thickener, this gives a subtle glossy finish to sauces. Cornstarch will also substitute.

rakkyō (pickled scallions)
Small round, white pickles, these are a kind of scallion, usually pickled in sweetened vinegar or a mixture of *mirin* and soy sauce. *Rakkyō* are often set out together with *fukujin-zuke* red pickles when Japanese-style curry is served.

rāyu
Chinese hot chili oil, available in small bottles in Asian markets.

rice
In Japan, the rice used is short-grain. With Japanese food, it's best to use short- or medium-grain rice, if possible, since these grains have a sticky quality that makes them perfect for eating with chopsticks. Short- and medium-grain are readily available in Asian markets and supermarkets.

In recipes in which white rice is simply eaten as an accompaniment to a dish, it is fine to use instant rice.

rice vinegar
See vinegar.

saké
Known as rice wine, this beverage is actually produced by brewing. It is sold in liquor stores and, in some areas, in Asian markets and supermarkets. *See also mirin.*

sanshō Japanese pepper
This is a brownish spice, not really hot, but rather tangy and aromatic. It is used mainly with chicken and eel. Available at Asian markets.

satoimo
See field yams.

satsumaimo
See sweet potato.

sesame (*goma*)
This is used in the forms of oil, paste, and seeds.

Sesame oil subtly enriches a dish without overwhelming the basic flavor. It will keep indefinitely if stored away from direct sunlight. For Japanese cooking it is best to use Japanese brands.

Sesame seeds are available in white and black varieties. White are used in a greater variety of dishes, but the flavor is much the same. Black seeds are used raw, while white may be bought either roasted or raw; the raw white seeds need to be roasted.

Sesame paste is available in Asian markets. Or substitute Middle Eastern tahini or any smooth, unsweetened nut butter, such as peanut butter.

shichimi tōgarashi ("seven-spice" chili powder)

Often simply called *shichimi*, Japanese seven-spice chili powder consists of hot chili pepper mixed with at least 6 other spices. The flavor varies depending upon the formula the maker uses. Regular chili powder will substitute.

In Japan, chili powder that is not mixed with other spices is called *ichimi* ("one-spice") *tōgarashi*.

shiitake mushrooms

Dark brown mushrooms with wide flat caps, short hard stems, and a distinctive, rich flavor. The stems are fibrous and tough, and are usually discarded. Shiitake are available both fresh and dried. The dried variety needs to be reconstituted by soaking in warm water until softened, about 10 minutes. Fresh shiitake are never eaten raw, but are used in all types of cooked and grilled dishes.

shimeji mushrooms (oyster mushrooms)

Available fresh at some Asian markets, these have a pleasant, light flavor. Brown in color, they are joined at the base of the stems into a cluster. Other kinds of mushrooms, including button mushrooms, will substitute.

shirataki (white filament konnyaku)

This version of *konnyaku* consists of thin white filaments. Like *konnyaku*, it is made of paste from the devil's tongue plant and has no calories. It is sold fresh, packed in water.

shishito sweet green pepper

This small pepper looks like a jalapeño, but the taste is mild and sweet. In size it is very close to okra.

shiso

See perilla leaves.

shūmai wrappers

Square wrappers, sold in stacks wrapped in plastic in the refrigerator case in Asian markets. Wonton wrappers are thicker, but can substitute if necessary.

soy sauce (shōyu)

Dark salty liquid that is a mainstay of Asian cooking. It is a mixture of soybeans, wheat, and water that is naturally fermented, aged, and distilled. For Japanese cooking, be sure to look for the Japanese kind, not the Chinese, since the flavors are quite different.

Some recipes in this book call for *usukuchi*, or light-colored soy sauce, which like white pepper is used to keep the overall color of certain dishes light. However, this is actually higher in sodium than regular soy sauce. If light-colored soy sauce is not available, regular soy sauce can be substituted; see the equivalent measures given in each recipe.

In the United States there is also a product called "lite" soy sauce, which is low-sodium. This should not be confused with *usukuchi* (light-colored) soy sauce.

sudachi (Japanese lime)

This small and acidic citrus fruit is sometimes referred to as a Japanese lime. When ripe, it actually becomes yellow, like the Japanese *yuzu* citron. *Sudachi* is used when it is dark green, however, and still unripe.

sugar

When a recipe in this book calls for sugar, this refers to granulated white sugar.

sweet potato (satsumaimo)

This is very close to the sweet potato that is familiar in the United States, although the Japanese variety is a bit sweeter and the texture is firmer. American sweet potatoes or yams can be substituted.

tōbanjan

See Chinese spicy miso-chili paste.

tofu

Tofu is an inexpensive protein alternative to meat. It has been eaten in Japan for centuries and is now becoming popular around the world. It is available in two types—firm, or "cotton" (in Japanese, *momen-dōfu*) and soft, or "silken" (*kinu-dōfu*). It is readily available in most large supermarkets, Asian markets, and natural food stores.

Abura-age, or deep-fried slice of tofu, is a rich golden brown color. Before use, some people prefer to reduce the oil content by holding briefly under hot running water and squeezing. Available in the refrigerator case in Asian markets.

tōgarashi
See shichimi tōgarashi.

trefoil (*mitsuba*)
This herb, a member of the parsley family, appears frequently in Japanese cooking. It is often used as a garnish, both for its decorative green color and for its piquant flavor.

udon noodles
Thick white wheat noodles available at Asian markets. Dried noodles will store almost indefinitely.

usukuchi soy sauce
See soy sauce.

vinegar
The vinegar usually used in Japan is white rice vinegar, mild in taste and made from fermented glutinous rice. It is available in Asian markets and in some supermarkets. Any white vinegar—wine, cider, etc.—will substitute.

wakame seaweed
Found in the dried foods section in Asian markets, this is a dark green, brownish color. When reconstituted, however, it becomes a rich, bright green. It is one of the most nutritious of sea vegetables, and it has no calories.

yakisoba noodles
Made from wheat and eggs, *yakisoba* noodles are used only for fried noodle dishes. They may be available fresh in vacuum-sealed packs in the refrigerator section of Asian markets and should not be confused with *soba* noodles, which are made from buckwheat.

yuzu (Japanese citron)
Yuzu is used almost exclusively for its aromatic rind, tiny shavings of which are used to season soups and to flavor simmered dishes. Lemon will substitute, although lemon rind should be washed carefully before use.

Index ■

N

O

P

Acknowledgments

Editing: Elizabeth Ogata and Michiko Uchiyama
Translation: Erika Young
Book design: Kazuhiko Miki
Illustrations: Minori Mizukami (pages 9 and 88 and section symbols)
Line drawings: Tadamitsu Omori (pages 41, 43, 45, 61, 67, 69, 75, and 89)
Research: William Floyd

Photograph of lotus root on page 11 by Minowa Studio

Other photographs originally appeared in:

(Photographs by Shigeki Aoto of Kodansha Ltd., with styling by Norio Itai)
Kobayashi Katsuyo no okazu hyakka (Tokyo: Kodansha Ltd., 1999)
Kobayashi Katsuyo no yasashii washoku (Tokyo: Kodansha Ltd., 1995)
Kobayashi Katsuyo no yasashii osechi (Tokyo: Kodansha Ltd., 1995)
Kobayashi Katsuyo no yasashii men/pasta (Tokyo: Kodansha Ltd., 1997)
Kobayashi Katsuyo no yasashii kurisumasu ryōri (Tokyo: Kodansha Ltd., 1996)

(Photographs by Shigeki Aoto, with styling by Mariko Kawasaki)
Kobayashi Katsuyo juku (Tokyo: Kodansha Ltd., 1997 [vol. 1] and 1998 [vols. 2 and 3])

小林カツ代のホームクッキング
The Quick and Easy Japanese Cookbook

2000 年 7 月　第 1 刷発行
2006 年 4 月　第 6 刷発行

著　者　小林カツ代

発行者　富田　充

発行所　講談社インターナショナル株式会社
　　　　〒 112–8652 東京都文京区音羽 1–17–14
　　　　電話 03–3944–6493 （編集部）
　　　　　　 03–3944–6492 （マーケティング部・業務部）
　　　　ホームページ www.kodansha-intl.com

印刷・製本所　共同印刷株式会社

落丁本・乱丁本は購入書店名を明記のうえ、講談社インターナショナル業務部宛にお送りください。送料小社負担にてお取替えします。なお、この本についてのお問い合わせは、編集部宛にお願いいたします。本書の無断複写（コピー）、転載は著作権法の例外を除き、禁じられています。

定価はカバーに表示してあります。

© 小林カツ代 2000
Printed in Japan
ISBN 4–7700–2504–1